TAKING THE STRESS OUT OF LEADERSHIP!

A practical guide
to increasing well-being

Sue Firth

First edition written & printed 2018

Copyright © Sue Firth, 2018

ISBN: 978-0-9560029-3-8

A CIP Catalogue of this book is available from the British Library.

ALSO BY SUE FIRTH

'*More Life – Less Stress*' on e-book, and kindle

'*Taking the Stress out of Life*' audio download

'*How to Maximise Your Self-Esteem*' audio download

For more information on Sue Firth's books, audio and learning tools, please visit www.suefirthltd.com

FOREWORD

"Stress is certainly a modern-day issue that affects our lives and potentially our health. Too much stress, implying difficulties with handling pressures and coping with them, can have a cumulative 'negative effect' on our well-being. It has been implicated in contributing to heart disease and cancer plus many other disease syndromes including diabetes and obesity. It is therefore of great benefit to understand stress and its possible outcomes; learn to recognize key signs and symptoms that may be associated with it, and whenever possible be able to avoid any negative side effects before they develop into real health concerns. We think stress is important to identify as a risk factor and whenever possible to try and neutralize its harmful effects. This book provides some valuable insights into that and makes an important contribution towards optimizing health and well-being for the future".

Dr L Dorian Dugmore
President/Founder Wellness International
Nucleus Board Member for Sport Cardiology & Prevention, European Society of Cardiology

Working long hours ...

CONTENTS

INTRODUCTION

What is this book about?

Stress is a subject we hear a lot about these days. We often read about how much money stress is costing industry. This is in sickness benefit due to stress related illness or in lost man hours due to absenteeism. Recent figures from the Health & Safety Executive, state that absenteeism due to stress amounts to 105 million days/year. This equals £1.24 billion in the U.K. In the U.S the figures are even higher. They experience 550 million working days lost to stress related absenteeism. This cost an estimated $200 billion per year! That amounts to a lot of money.

Yet, there are two points to make here:

Point No. 1

Media representation has spread the message that stress is a negative experience. An illness almost, from which most of us will suffer at some time. *FACT: Stress is not an illness, but it can exacerbate existing illness.* This might make some of us feel almost everything is stressful! In fact, stress is only a negative experience if you *perceive* the situation as stressful for you. Thus, two people can experience the same event but one of them feels it is negative and the other manageable. As individuals our personalities vary and our previous experiences differ. So does what we have learnt about how capable we are and about what matters to us. All this plays a part in how we 'filter' situations and how we choose to react.

Stress is a natural reaction and it will continue to be with us for a long time to come.

Point No. 2

It is completely unreasonable to assume that stress explains the rise in the figures. There are many circumstances that contribute to this statistic. Stress is not an illness. You can experience an increased risk of illness by *believing* that your life is stressful. We will talk more about exactly what stress is in Chapter 1 but, in general, it is a natural reaction. We experience it whenever we experience threat. Yet is the state of the nation's health that we also need to look at.

We need to acknowledge that many of us we are more sedentary than we've ever been. We eat refined carbohydrates, live on caffeine, and look for stimulants to cope. This is the bigger picture. Our lifestyle choices are important. They contribute to insufficient exercise, excess fat and an over-secretion of insulin. This in turn, leads to an increased chance of illness.

Modern living surrounds us with pressures to conform, and perform. Our reaction to these pressures results in how well we cope. The demands are external to us, such as work deadlines. They are also 'internal' as our lifestyle can trigger stress. If we decide to eat a barrage of sugar, fat and drink caffeine we *may* be adding to the problem.

Recognising *whether* you are stressed is the first step. Then we need to identify your symptoms and understand their significance. At that stage simple lifestyle changes might be all you need. If those don't solve the problem, you could analyse the triggers or sources of stress. Then you determine how your own personality influences how much stress you feel. Followed by how well you cope. Any one of these stages can mitigate the effects of stress

What are you going to get from this book?

The book is full of explanation, suggestions, and advice. There are seven chapters, each with a core body of information. There is a 'Tips section' to help you reduce the stress you experience as soon as you can. There are practical or pragmatic suggestions for you to put into practice immediately. There are points which are 'Food for Thought'. These may not have occurred to you, but they could be contributing to your stress. Each section is there to help you.

To recap: we cannot eradicate stress, nor should we expect to, but we can go a long way towards helping ourselves handle it well. In fact, many of us thrive on it!

Stress may happen by accident or by design. Stress management cannot happen by accident. We need to make a determined and committed effort to affect our stress. We all need support and this book helps you find it.

Very best wishes,

Sue Firth *BSc Hons, MSc*
Business Psychologist, Stress expert, Author, and Speaker
Consulting Rooms:58 South Molton St, London
www.suefirthltd.com

Associate Fellow of the British Psychological Society (BPS). Member of the Health & Care Professions Council (HCPC)

1 WHAT IS STRESS?

Stress is a natural and normal reaction. We all experience it. Being alive in a modern world surrounds us with stimuli and the need to respond. Many of these demands have become the 'norm' so we forget (or do not realise), how much they can affect our health. The issue, is what I call 'hidden stress'. This is the frequency with which stress alters our immune system.

Adrenaline is amazing and many Executives I work with remark that they thrive on it. It's a complicated hormone that speeds up your body. There is only one reason for this; your brain must be able to get your body out of danger whenever it is necessary. In some cases, the danger is an oncoming car. These 'demands' are manageable and may be short lived. The 'hidden stress' comes from feeling the need to respond to a range of situations. So, we become mobilised for fight or flight for very long periods of time. A mother who fights the traffic to drop her children off at school has had a tough start to the day and it's only just begun! Executives are the same. They start the day by looking at their phone before even leaving the house. Other external demands continue throughout the day without respite. This pushes their body to respond.

But, there are three points to make. First, we are often not under physical threat, but we may be under mental or *emotional* pressure. Our brains cannot tell the difference. Our thoughts trigger this reaction as much as any physical threat.

Second, we are experiencing the 'Stress response' far more than we may need. We can underestimate the impact of that. Then we assume that the adrenal glands have an infinite capacity to respond. This isn't so. It is also a misconception when some people say they don't experience stress at all. What they mean, is they do not recognise the stress as a *negative problem.* That may be an interesting difference in their personality or way of thinking. In fact, everyone experiences stress. It is a physical impossibility not to have experienced it at some time

Third, because you experience it doesn't make it bad! Your body copes well but modern-day living demands that we may cope well. Unless we can influence how we view the demands *or compensate for them* we may not do so. Research shows that it is *not* the situation that is the issue, but our reaction *to it* that matters. This is what we have real control over! So, stress management works best when it involves the management of adrenaline/cortisol. This has to involve the management of our thoughts. That way, we take control

You will know when you are living on cortisol when you wake up every day. Your muscles (particularly your shoulder and neck muscles), will be tense.

This makes you feel as if you've done ten rounds in a boxing ring! Consistent stress management techniques can help dissipate this tension. It is better to include habits that help prevent it from being there in the first place too.

What does the Stress Response do?

The stress response impacts five essential areas of your body. These five are the same for all of us. Some of us may experience specific reactions to these changes too. The five areas are as follows:

HEART Your heart rate increases thus pumping more blood around the body. This blood contains adrenaline and the oxygen needed to supply vital organs. It also contains sugars which help feed those organs with essential nutrients. This is so that they can work faster.

LUNGS Your lungs increase their capacity to take in air. The increased rate of oxygen uptake is now pumped faster out of the heart

MUSCLES Your muscles contract ready for action. A supply of sugar within the muscle begins to help them move. This means you can move as fast as your physical fitness and build will allow. Muscles need practice at moving to do this well. That's one of the reasons we recommend that you exercise.

BRAIN Your brain now transmits billions of signals across the cells. These signals trigger an increased speed of response to the threat to get you out of danger.

STOMACH Your digestion process turns OFF. This is a non-essential activity for survival. Your brain believes that you do not need to digest food in your stomach nor do you have the capacity to digest it. This suggests that the adrenaline reaction was only ever meant to be a short-term action

So, what have we learned?

So far, I've explained that the stress response is essential to survival. It gal-vanises a system that is working but does not need to operate fast unless we encounter a threat. The slow 'ticking over' of our bodies when we are not moving or not doing much is homeostasis. This is like a car on idle: every-thing working but without pressure. Once adrenaline enters our bodies, adrenaline kick-starts it to react. The car engine now accelerates. Every-thing from the pistons to the petrol consumption, goes up!

The issue for those who want peak performance is that the frequency of stress puts pressure on our body. We are often not aware of the impact of that. Being alert for long periods without respite, places a strain on the adrenals to supply. It was not designed to do this for long periods of time. Extreme demands over a prolonged period cause inflammation in our bod-ies. Inflammation suppresses the immune system. The result, is often symp-toms of stress that seem unrelated. Difficulty in sleeping, repeated colds, or low testosterone are examples. The latter is a direct result of our bodies undergoing something called a 'cortisol steal'. We need to use LDL cho-lesterol to make cortisol over testosterone. Our bodies use the same sub-stance to make both but prioritise one over the other when under stress. Men may find this interesting! Not having enough respect for stress is an important point. It means some executives do not appreciate that they are experiencing hard lives.

I also find Executives are *attracted* to a role that carries a certain amount of stress within it. Top jobs are tough both from making decisions and the *impact* of those decisions. Demands from cash flow, and the consequences of decisions can weigh on someone. When I ask a group of Executives why they do the job they do, many of them reflect. They reply that the excite-ment, autonomy, growth, and opportunities for success are it. These are all great reasons. But they ALL stimulate your body, and this stimulation triggers adrenaline. Many of the Executives have been doing this for so long they *expect* it and find it normal. But our bodies have not evolved well for this long-term exposure. Modification of our lives might be part of the answer. We need to allow for down-time, rest, and respite from the adrenaline rush. This is essential for long term maintenance of our bodies that will otherwise tend to crash.

Executives also like control. Nothing comes as more of a shock than finding their own body does not respond well to persistent demands. The day they cannot get out of bed or find they *don't want to* comes as a shock. But this wear and tear is a sure sign they've overdone it. Repairing this is possible but takes time. Losing time on the job especially at a busy period is *very* frustrating. It is better to change your lifestyle in time than do it later. Simple, repeatable, consistent steps give your body a chance. Experiencing that flat feeling is adrenal burn out and this takes longer to treat.

1. Food for Thought!

Our brains cannot tell the difference between a vividly imagined and a real event.

When you feel anxious or negative about it, it's likely that your thoughts are negative. If your thinking is negative, then you could trigger the stress response. Anxiety about a forthcoming meeting or a client who is difficult, adds up.

The significance of this is that the *anticipation* of events is as likely to generate stress in us. Not only do we rev up *before* an event, but also *during* it and after. If you replay events in your mind *after* they have occurred, this too can generate stress.

The adrenal response is sensitive to emotional triggers. Any event that is, or was, significant to you, will can release adrenaline but is also emotional. This might be why stress has a bad name. For some they recover from an experience, then the *anticipation of* a second event triggers stress again.

2. Our thoughts have a massive effect on us!

Our brains cannot tell the difference between imagined and real events. Both are able to trigger the stress response. Our *thoughts* can also trigger the stress response. We do not have to be near a situation to feel an intense 'hit' from adrenaline, pumped in out of fun, fear, or anticipation. The solution might be that we need to learn to *control our thoughts.* There are over 2000 electrical impulses experienced every second in our brains. They control what is happening in our bodies. Counsellors and Life Coaches often spend a great deal of time trying to fix our thoughts. That is because consistent, negative thoughts about ANYTHING in life can stimulate adrenaline. This isn't good for us, but the key is to recognise that life *can* be demanding although it can also be fun!

3. Many of us are not active enough to dissipate the adrenaline in our body.

At one time as a species we worked for a living using manual labour. Working in this way was a good release for adrenaline. That's because the physical movement this created dissipated the fight or flight response. It might seem obvious but if we move more, we use the muscles that are tense and feel more relaxed as a result. Instead, we are using appliances to help streamline our lives. Computers, television, radio, and video games are appliances. They reduce our need to fill recreational hours with physical activity. Mobile phones in particular, encourage us to work for very long periods of time but often sat down.

We are all encouraged to exercise more to protect our hearts and to reduce stress. Yet many executives I work with will tell me that they don't have the time. Prioritising movement in our lives is important and doesn't have to be onerous. Going to the gym might be desirable, but 2 x 15-minute walks/ day break up your working day. They increase your energy levels and give your brain a much-needed break.

2 LOOKING FOR SYMPTOMS

Because we all experience stress as a matter of everyday living, it is likely we will experience some symptoms of stress too. One specialist put it well when he said:

"If you use a system that has evolved in 99% of beasts on this planet for dealing with a three-minute crisis and turn it on for 30 years worrying about a mortgage, then what you get is a constant switch 'on' of the stress response. It simply didn't evolve for this and the body pays a price"

—Dr Robert Sapolsky

Some symptoms of stress are quite acceptable as long as they are mild or short lived. If they are treatable such as the odd headache, or period of sleeplessness that too is fine. Even mild anxiety is ok, but it helps if you determine if a symptom is 'significant' or not. Typical symptoms are important too. If you are sleeping well, have regular moods, and cope well with most situations, then this is good. It's also good to laugh but if you're not smiling much this is important.

The following questionnaire is one method we designed as a company. It is not exhaustive, but will help you identify your symptoms of stress.

A QUICK QUESTIONNAIRE ON STRESS

Think about how you would answer each of these questions. 'Always' means this behaviour is typical of you). 'Sometimes' means you *can* be this way but you just as often don't feel like it. 'Rarely' means you almost never experience it.

1.   Do you find that you are easily irritable?

2.   Do you lose your temper easily?

3.   Do you suffer from tension headaches?
        Do you feel tired and have no energy?

4.   Are you physically tense?

5.   Do you feel you can't see the wood from the trees?

6.   Do you feel very dissatisfied with your home life?

7.   Do you feel very dissatisfied with your work life?

8.   Are your relationships with people strained and difficult?

9. Are you unable to relax?

10. Have you stopped smiling?

11. Do you worry a lot?

12. Do you feel you lack confidence?

13. Do you think you don't feel good about yourself as a person?

14. Do you think you can't express yourself or your feelings to anyone?

15. Do you find situations overwhelming?

16. Do you find difficulty in coping with life?

If you answered 'always' to a question, then score 2. If you answered 'sometimes', then score 1 and if you answered, 'rarely or never', score 0. Total your score and look at the interpretation below. These are the recommendations we make depending on your score:

0 – 10: You are thriving on life! It may not be particularly stressful. You could be coping well with one or two situations, or not aware of much distress in your life at the moment. Keep up the good work but try to make sure you get enough time to yourself as well as any commitments you may have.

11 – 20: You are likely experience mild stress. This may suggest there may be *some* difficult situations you are experiencing now. If you feel you are handling these quite well or you can see the light at the end of the tunnel, then brilliant. If your Stress continues for some time your symptoms are likely to deepen or worsen. You may wish to re-take the questionnaire in a few months to check.

21 – 30: The questionnaire indicates you may be experiencing significant stress. If you have not been aware of this, try to consider the information has helped you 'see' the situation better. Seek advice to reduce your stress

levels or moderate your lifestyle. If you have been aware of the stress you're under, set yourself a target for how long you will tolerate it. Determine if there is *anything* at all you can do to improve the situation for yourself.

This book has a lot of tips and guidance, so it might be a good first step. If nothing changes for you then you may be better to seek someone to talk to and advice you. They may help you get some perspective and support you better. A Psychologist coach, or counsellor (depending on the severity of the problem), may be best

What next? The Chemistry of Performance

The following exercise is one I use with every Executive group I work with. It is an interesting and valuable tool. It helps them identify where they are experiencing stress but also the impact it is having.

To start: take a blank piece of paper and draw a vertical line in the middle of the page about 10 cms long. Put the words 'Active' at the top and 'Relaxed' at the bottom. This is the way your body reacts to daily life. Underneath the word 'Active' write the word *Adrenaline*. Underneath the word 'Relaxed', write the word *Serotonin*.

The Chemistry of Performance

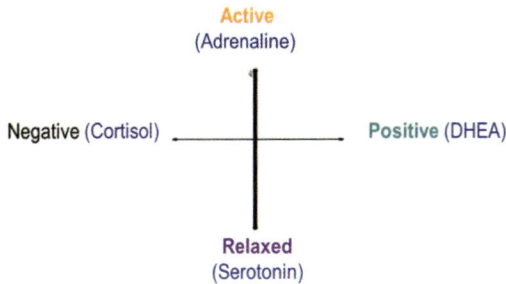

Active
(Adrenaline)

Negative (Cortisol) ⟵————————⟶ Positive (DHEA)

Relaxed
(Serotonin)

© Sue Firth Ltd 2017

Serotonin is important. It is an essential brain hormone responsible for appetite and mood. It is also found in the gut, in fact 80% of it is there.

The horizontal line influences our mood. This ranges from a negative mood which may involve stress. Then Cortisol is made. Being positive about a situation triggers the introduction of DHEA (or Dehydroepiandrosterone). Each of these hormones has an impact on us but there are some key points to make about the significance of them.

1. If we look at the top right quadrant, we describe the behaviours that go with that state. This is you on an adrenaline high. Most people would say they feel a buzz, an energised productive rush. This helps them get things done and they feel happy. They are busy and feel good.

2. The bottom right quadrant is a happy, but relaxed state. When you feel like this you look calm, feel 'chilled' and soothed. If these feelings seem unfamiliar then you may not be getting enough time to relax. Although it may be less frequent, this is a very productive place to be. It's likely that the parasympathetic nervous system is active here.

3. The top left quadrant is the one that describes an unhappy, adrenaline high. The symptoms here indicative of a negative state of stress. This person is experiencing the side effects of Cortisol. Here people would describe feeling grumpy, irritable, frustrated and prone to anger. This is a vicious circle that is difficult to break at the time you're feeling it. We all know how hard it is to stop feeling irritable, but it pays to try. This is because Cortisol aggravates your system and perpetuates the problem. This leaves you prone to making mistakes, whether verbal errors or real ones. It also makes us prone to upsetting our relationships, whether at home or at work.

4. The bottom left quadrant is an unhappy, anxious state. It is symptomatic of not enough Serotonin in our brain and body. It describes a negative change that can range from being lethargic to apathetic. More serious symptoms show depression. When you or someone you know starts to behave out of character this is the start of a change. If their appearance changes or they withdraw from life and talk less they could be very unhappy. take time off and generally seem less able to cope. They may need support to get themselves out of that state. If you have been there too it's important to recognise it. It's also important to tackle it early and it is quite workable to do it. It is possible to do this without counselling if you observe it early. It is more likely to be successful if you tackle the chemical changes whilst they are not yet imbalanced. Depression is a chemical change as well as a lifestyle issue. It means there is a route for improving your mood by adjusting your body and brain chemistry. Then you introduce simple strategies to alter your habits. Tackling both by understanding your physiology is a vital strategy

The Chemistry of Performance

	Active (Adrenaline)	
Irritable		Happy
Grumpy		Hyper
Angry		Buzz
Negative (Cortisol)		Positive (DHEA)
Lethargic		Happy
Apathetic		Relaxed
Depressed	Relaxed (Serotonin)	Calm

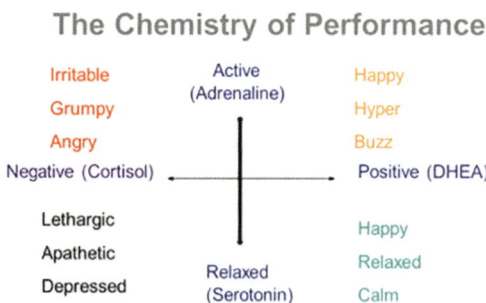

© Sue Firth Ltd 2013

There are a few questions to ask yourself in the following exercise. Do this before moving on to how you can adjust and change your body or brain chemistry to help you feel good.

a. Decide what percentage out of 100 you spend in each state or quadrant during a typical week? This includes work and home life but not sleep.

b. Then ask, what were your percentages a year ago? Take a longer time in the past if you need, but put these in brackets higher up on each quadrant

c. Now ask yourself, in general, have the scores improved or worsened in that time?

d. What is the biggest explanation for the difference in the scores?

e. Ask yourself what situations & which people, put you on the right-hand side of the map?

f. Who or what puts you on the left-hand side? (These could be quite revealing, and sometimes are the same people!)

g. Then draw the numbers 1 to 5 spaced out on the horizontal axis on the right. Draw the numbers -1 to -5 on the left-hand side. Where do you find yourself getting out of bed in the morning and where do you end your day? Then draw an arrow in the direction of change you tend to take. So, do you start as a 3 and end as a -3 or begin at a -1 but end at a 4?

The following diagram is an example of this.

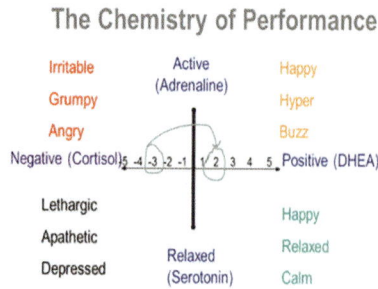

The Chemistry of Performance

Irritable	Active (Adrenaline)	Happy
Grumpy		Hyper
Angry		Buzz

Negative (Cortisol) -5 -4 -3 -2 -1 | 1 2 3 4 5 Positive (DHEA)

Lethargic		
Apathetic		Happy
Depressed	Relaxed (Serotonin)	Relaxed
		Calm

What to do next:

Your percentages are not an exact science. As a rough guide, spending around 30% to 40% of your time in the top right would help you feel good. More than that and you'll 'burn' adrenalin as fuel, but it isn't a fuel and the adrenals can get tired. Your body doesn't make it as jet fuel. It makes it to ensure survival. Living on a chemical designed for periods of peak activity without enough rest, is a recipe for burn out.

Like a car, the bottom right quadrant represents having your foot on the brake or stopping for petrol. You wouldn't run an expensive Ferrari without filling it up yet we often try to keep going whilst running on empty! The lower right 'state' deserves respect so stats of approx. 30% to 40% would be good here. It is curious how many Executives view this as a negative place and think of it as a boring place to be. In fact, activities that involve Serotonin are soothing and likely to be sustainable. They represent emotions that evoke something more creative. This includes drawing, writing, or playing with your kids on the floor. This is **not** a high energy state, but it is an easier one to live in. It's also important for protecting you. It counteracts the negative effects of prolonged exposure to stress. Being on an adrenalin 'high' has its benefits but also its drawbacks. Many of these are likely to come about if an Executive isn't enjoying their work.

The top left quadrant is best lived in for short periods of time as it's likely to be very exacting. You can end up wired and tired here. Only aim for 10% or 20% because this is a high energy state. It is one where you are feeling upset, so you may lose your temper or feel strained. Higher stats than these might need support. This may be to help you manage anger or it may be life is carrying a cost right now. You could be paying the price and bringing it out on loved ones as your irritation blows in to anger. Anger is ok on an infrequent basis, but not good all the time. As you 'blow up' the lava you leave behind can do damage to others both in the workplace, and at home.

The bottom left is obvious once you start looking at it. 5% or 10% is best here. We all experience periodic upset, fatigue, or tiredness. Consistent or persistent sadness though, leads to withdrawal and anxiety.

Excessive time in here carries a risk of sliding further. Depression is best treated with a combination of support and medication

To use this information ask yourself:

a. If your stats were different a year ago, analyse the explanation for the difference. Check them out with your loved ones. Ask them about how your behaviour has changed rather than relying on your view. You are looking for a gentle reality check here. If you know you blow up at work then try to recognise the damage you are doing to yourself *and* to them.

b. People and situations that put you on the right are good. Repeat these if possible, and those that put you on the left, avoid them wherever you can. Although that sounds easy to say and difficult to do, think of it this way. They are gains and drains for you. If you prefer, see them as deposits and withdrawals

c. The horizontal axis and the number you would apply, is significant. Your family are *feeling the impact* of that in a negative way if your mood is unhappy in the mornings. Needing your own space or taking time to wake up, are both normal so starting the day in the negative end may be fine. Ending it on that side might not be good. If you felt positive at the beginning of the day but felt negative at the end of it then you could be unhappy. It may warrant a good, look at the explanations for that. You may want to tackle this with the tools from chapter 3. You could break down the sources and causes of stress outlined in chapters 4 and 5. The main point of the chemistry map is to see it as you would a bank account. The right-hand side is the 'deposits' you make to the bank and the left is the 'withdrawals. If you make too many withdrawals and not enough deposits, the account will be in overdraft. The deficit can be unsustainable. No self-respecting business man or woman would operate a business in the red. Yet we do this to ourselves all the time!

Conclusions

A business that is in the red would reflect on the owner or manager of it. Even when it's not their fault, the discomfort of this can make them feel a failure. The chemistry map is very similar in that if you live in deficit it drains the system. This leaves you with an increased likelihood or risk of slipping further. With chemical changes, this alteration can lead to depression and low self-esteem. Men I have noticed, lose their self-respect when in this space. They either find it hard to come out, because of their lack of experience, or fight hard to come out but need support. Unless you understand *where* you are, and *how* you've got there, you may find it difficult to know what to do. Without the tools to know what to do next, some people can struggle. Much of the book emphasises the tools you can use but it also highlights the benefit of seeking advice.

N. B. When you feel unhappy, Cortisol hits your system. There can be a 15-minute delay between your exposure to an event though, and the chemical change. This might not sound long, but if use it to your advantage, you can learn to calm down. This can prevent the worst of the Cortisol hit. That way you develop the resilience to tackle the situation in hand. This avoids reacting too fast, or over-reacting. Overreacting can result in causing offence or drawing attention to ourselves. I once sat near a man in a train carriage who grew very angry. The train kept coming to a halt as it travelled the last few miles of the journey from where I lived to central London. The guard kept apologising and explained there was a problem on the line. This was affecting every train trying to enter the station. The man kept swearing. The change in his body language and physical language was plain to see. I could almost feel the moment the Cortisol hit his system and his irritation became anger. Then he exploded in temper and ran off the train. He almost collided with passengers walking towards the stationary train.

You can see this kind of change in physiological state in all sorts of situations. It is Cortisol that explains why a mother can reach the stage of smacking a youngster who will not do as they're told. The perpetual struggle to keep calm loses to the inevitable irritation that follows. Undeterred, the youngster persists in misbehaving. A sharp smack ensues but it is quite likely to be the rise in Cortisol that explains it. It reduces her resources to handle the situation.

The following chapter describes the strategies you can use that alter your chemistry. Although not as useful for intense and tough situations in life, they can support you. If you shift your chemistry for the better, situations can feel easier to handle. Later chapters handle moderate to severe stress.

3 Supporting Your Chemistry and Symptoms of Stress

To handle stress, we need to learn to 'manage our state' or mood. Handling adrenaline or Cortisol is the key to managing short term, immediate stress. It underpins the strategy for the long-term management of stress. For this there are other tactics that you use. I will come to these in the next chapters

The most immediate thing is to learn to manage stress better so that you can feel 'in control of it'. This is better than 'being controlled *by* it'.

What to do next:

After scoring the stress questionnaire, you have an idea about your stress. What you may like to do now is follow these guidelines to prioritise. This will determine which symptoms are the most important to target for improvement.

Begin by rewriting the top symptoms from your questionnaire. Those are the ones you answered 'Always' to. If you have none, then rewrite the ones you answered 'Sometimes' to. Now you need to ask yourself three questions as follows:

How often do I get this symptom?

How bad or significant is it for me?

How long does this symptom last?

What these questions do is help you decide which symptom to tackle first. Your responses show the 'frequency', 'intensity' and 'duration' of your symptom. If you answered that you feel it often, it's quite bad and lasts a long time, then you may need to decide two things. *What* is the single biggest contributing factor to that symptom? Is it something or someone? Can you alter this or moderate it at all? Do you currently do enough to relieve this symptom? Can you think of anything else you could do to moderate it?

Are you reaching for the right kind of help? We often self-diagnose our stress and self-medicate it. Taking over-the-counter pain relief is ok if not excessive. You can become addicted to non-prescription medication though. The side-effects of that mimic the same symptoms you're trying to treat so chat to your Dr if you worry about this

Examples of significant symptoms that may need help to improve:

- Feeling persistently unhappy

- Not taking holidays

- Working every weekend

- Working long hours because you believe you must

- Finding your social life hard work and wanting to avoid people

- Confusion, distress or feeling overwhelmed

- An increase in physical, emotional, or psychological symptoms – e.g. a cold becomes persistent, a one-off stomach upset remains a problem. Or you start personalising events believing you are at fault or to blame for everything

Any symptoms you feel are manageable and don't occur often, or are generally fine. Coping with your symptoms and still living life to the full is critical to your well-being. For example, I give presentations for a living. I have low blood pressure and a tendency towards hypoglycaemia or low blood sugar too. This means I have an increased risk of headaches due to my sensitivity to going without food.

Travelling, poor sleep and long working hours, contribute to fewer opportunities to eat. I also struggle at times to get enough rest than I'd like but I *know* this, so I can expect it. I also enjoy the work I do so these symptoms are manageable for me. Whatever you experience there is a lot you can do to help yourself. This is what's coming next.

The Four Principles: Introducing M.E.P.S.

To begin, let's understand something about the human body. Your body and brain chemistry drive your physiology. The diagram describes this. This in turn, affects the physical function of your body. This impacts how you are feeling and *that* drives what you are thinking. We read this diagram from the *top*, down but this isn't correct. Our physiology is critical to our thoughts and can make a significant difference. Small changes we make to our physiology makes a *direct* impact on our emotions and thoughts. Adjustments we make to our lifestyle, affect our biology. They have a massive impact on our health and that, in turn, affects our experience of stress.

At any stage of this process you can change your physiology for the better. You can also exacerbate your stress by feeling unhappy. This releases more Cortisol. Your thoughts can trigger adrenaline and Cortisol in to your body. T*hinking* about these events is enough to trigger stress. You will react *as if* you are in a threatening situation. So, it is possible to stress as a result of different triggers. Your aneed for survival when faced with threat, your feelings, AND your thoughts. These affect your physiology and that in turn, changes your state.

Most of us are impatient at heart, and it can be much more motivating to see quick results. Changing your physiology alters your experience of stress and puts YOU in control. It helps you stop feeling that life is controlling you.

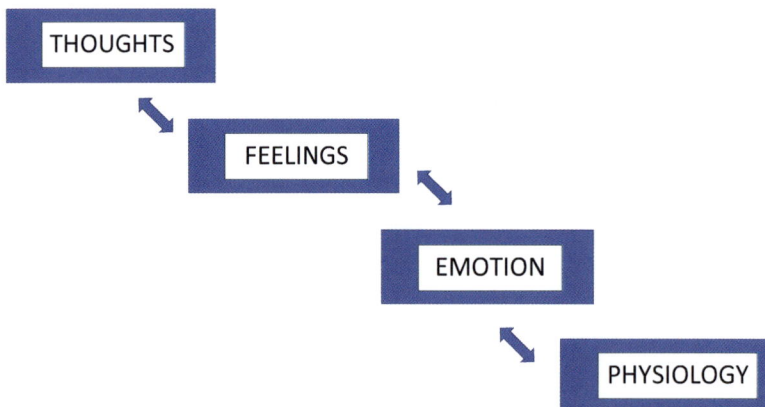

THOUGHTS

FEELINGS

EMOTION

PHYSIOLOGY

The First Principle: M for Mental

We will deal with your thoughts first. There are four simple suggestions here that alter your thinking for the better. These can influence how you respond or react to something.

1. Self-talk

We all talk to ourselves but a few of us recognise it is not a conscious process. It is as if our minds are active and 'full on'. This ongoing 'chat' can be destructive. This is especially if we are going through a tough phase of our lives (more on that in chapter 4).

When this happens, it is as if there are two versions of us inside our head – the good, or nice one, and the bad, or tough one. Studies conducted with children, suggest they hear 10 times more negative messages. In primary school they hear these more than positive ones. All children need to learn right from wrong, but repeated discipline is tough. Learning 'you can't' or 'don't do that', is difficult for us and we can learn not to try or believe we won't do well.

Yes, I did it!
I WILL DO IT
I CAN DO IT
I'LL TRY TO DO IT
HOW DO I DO IT?
I WANT TO DO IT
I CAN'T DO IT
I WON'T DO IT

WHICH STEP HAVE YOU REACHED TODAY?

When talking to groups I often ask if they are aware that they talk to themselves. Some put their hands up straight away. Others sit and ruminate for a bit. You can almost see the thought going through their mind "do I talk to myself, I don't know, do I?"

I have nicknamed these two voices the 'Shitty Committee'. Welcome to your shitty committee!! They are versions of you but they'll *feel* different. That might be because much of how the self talk has roots in our past. Teachers, parents and friends might have been angry or frustrated with us in the past. They use expressions like these.

Repeated, negative self-talk does harm. That's because it changes your cortisol levels, and the sympathetic nervous system. We end up with symptoms of stress. These include sleep difficulties, repeated colds and struggles with headaches and pains. These are quite likely to be coming from the same source. Your body feels under attack so we must learn to do something new. We need to learn to FIGHT BACK!

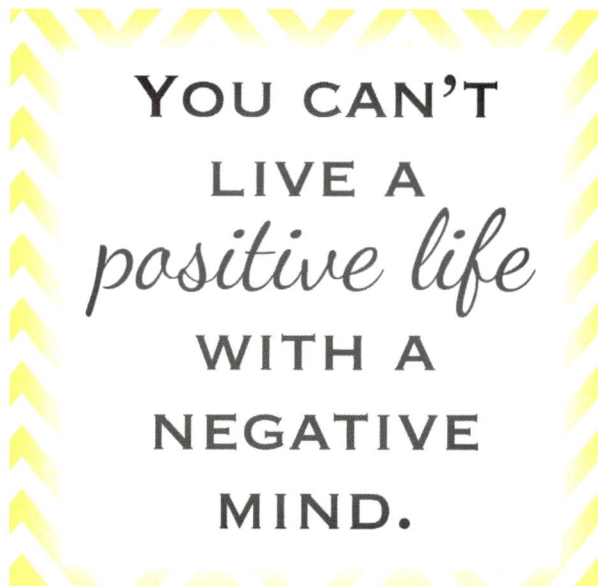

YOU CAN'T LIVE A *positive life* WITH A NEGATIVE MIND.

To fight back it is important to analyse the situation you're in. You might want to read chapters 6 onwards for ideas about how to do this but for now it can help to use a mantra.

A mantra is a series of simple, repeatable phrases. What these phrases are sometimes depends on the situation. It's a fair bet that the following might be good examples of a simple mantra to use:

I can manage this

I will find a way to solve this situation

I am doing my best

I have used three-line mantras like this with almost every client that comes in to see me in the practice. Many of them enjoy this simple technique. They use small A6 cards which they write on and carry the mantra around with them. Any situation they get into where they become unhappy they take out the card and read the mantra. Some even say it aloud!

It is also worth remembering; you will never talk to anyone as much as you talk to yourself. Please encourage that chat to be positive! I would not talk to others as I sometimes find I do to myself, it would be too harsh, so let's stop this habit now!

I also like to use motivational sayings such as this one which I have printed off and often look at on my desk.

Every thought
we think
is creating our future.

Louise Hay

2. Stillness, Meditation and Breathing

In a typical day there are benefits in being able to find a few short moments where you can sit still and breathe. Spending 5 to 10 minutes breathing a couple of times/day is valuable. This is particularly important without your phone or computer nearby. We are like a car that comes in for a pit stop and has its tyres changed. The human body needs a pause in the intensity with of a working day. To be fair, you would not work a horse or any other animal without letting it rest.

Taking a few minutes and sitting allows your mind to become conscious of breathing. This is a great mini pause in your day. I have a breathing technique that I like to teach which Dr Alan Watkins showed me. He uses a small piece of kit which helps measure your heart rate. Alan teaches that we all need to practice cardiac coherence. This is when our breathing slows to a rate where the electrical output of our heart becomes measured. That has both physical benefits, and physiological ones.

You can buy the earpiece which measures your heart rate from www.complete-coherence.com/coherence-heart-trainer/ and then you download the software from the site. It's easy to use and I have found it very valuable both to prove it to audiences but also for my own use. The benefits of this type of stillness, activates the parasympathetic nervous system. It engages the brain so that you can think straight, as opposed to feeling foggy headed and under stress. Whilst it won't change the situation you are experiencing, it does improve energy levels. This in turn, helps problem solve the situation at hand.

To learn the breathing technique is quite simple. All you do is breathe out for a count of five, pause for two, and breathe in for a count of five. We call this:

5 : 2 : 5

I practice this process several times in any one day. Although it works well if you are listening to your favourite piece of music or walking at the same time. What you are doing is also a form of

TOTAL FOCUS

and this is significant. When you focus on one thing at once your body cannot multitask and you are less stressed as a result.

Children stay focused when they are doing anything they enjoy. From building Lego to making a model plane, they sometimes seem in their own world. In fact, they are focussing and this gives our bodies and brain respite. The intense stimulation of our modern world and our modern way of working, seems to demand a lot from us.

Meditation is another very good example of this. If you know how to meditate then doing so twice a day for a few minutes each time is good. This will calm the constant chatter in your head. For the same reasons as being still has for both the body and mind, meditation is good for you. If you don't know how to meditate but would like to try it, download the app Headspace https://www.headspace.com/. Set your phone to the same time every day as this is beneficial. If you would prefer coaching to learn it, you could contact Katie Sheen at http:// www.soulnutrition.org/. Her expertise in mindfulness may help.

Relaxing is something many of us do not do well. If you can practice these two techniques, then you are likely to provide respite, for your body. When you have more time in the evening or at the weekend, take up a calmer hobby. Try being more creative or involve your kids. They find it easier to relax because they are not yet in bad habits!

3. Serotonin and Mood

Serotonin is a much-needed hormone that regulates our appetite and our mood. It releases at the onset of daylight and helps us stay calm and happy for much of the day. When Serotonin levels drop, we can become less calm and more anxious.

Several factors affect Serotonin levels. How much sleep we get makes a difference because we manufacture Serotonin at night. Busy Executives get less sleep when they're stressed so production of this substance can alter. The solution, is to do anything you can to ensure a good night's rest. More on that later in the chapter.

The next suggestion is to make sure you get some exercise during the day outside in the daylight. 2×15-minute walks/day are a great way of both lifting your energy levels and giving you a break. Daylight triggers serotonin within your brain and this gives your mood a boost. Sunlight is especially good for you. When you are on holiday it often has a soothing effect.

Other things you can do to boost production of serotonin would include the foods you eat. There is an enzyme we need to make serotonin in our gut and that is five hydroxy tryptophan or 5HTP for short. Foods which have this substance in it include: all the white meats such as chicken and turkey. Nuts, milk, bananas, high cocoa chocolate, oats, beans, lentils, and eggs are also sources. If you can, try to factor some of these foods in a daily basis.

Finally, light therapy is a great idea particularly if you go through a series of very dull days in the winter. Light therapy comes in the form of a Lightbox. Purchasing a lightbox is good even if you do not experience struggles with your mood in winter. I often use mine and turn it on approximately 30 minutes/day from the end of October until around the end of March. Living in the UK can mean there are a series of quite dull or overcast days. Using the lightbox gives me a short but valuable lift in mood that lasts the rest of the day.

You can buy these light boxes from large branches of Boots the chemist, John Lewis and online from www.lumie.com. I use the Brightspark which currently retails at £115 but there is also a desk lamp version. This might be quite useful because you could sit and do your emails whilst also getting a boost of light!

Low Serotonin levels can be tough and feel tiring or sad. This is the state symptomatic of the lower left on your chemistry map. Whilst we may experience this at some stage in our lives, spending prolonged time in here can feel tough. One-off or short-lived events, are unlikely to create an issue long term. That is unless they are unforeseen or traumatic. If you feel tired, sad, and unable to motivate yourself to work or socialise, this can be different. Symptoms of depression are important both for yourselves and for your employees.

These may include:

- Feeling sad or "empty"

- Feeling hopeless, irritable, anxious, or angry.

- Loss of interest in work, family, or once-pleasurable activities, including sex.

- Feeling very tired.

- Not being able to concentrate or remember details.

- Not being able to sleep or sleeping too much.

In these circumstances it is important for someone to seek help. There is more information on this in chapter 6. Counsellors are available by contacting your own healthcare insurance. You can also search for a Psychologist through the British Psychological Society.

Finding as counsellor who operates in your geographical area is www.bps.org.uk. Anyone can ask for help from their own GP too. Primary healthcare trusts can be under pressure to provide these services. and take longer to support someone.

4. Stimulation and Addiction

Computers, technology, and our mobile phones are amazing. They also make us available to others 24:7. This has its benefits and its downsides. Amongst the benefits are the fact that we can surf the net for almost any piece of information we ever want to know. Sitting watching a short film clip or video may give us respite in the right context, but there is a downside. We can find ourselves in 'checking mode' throughout the day.

Setting up notifications on your phone so that it pings at you end is a distraction and a fascination. We are keen to know who's been in touch and what they want. When we read something good it can help us to feel good. If we read something negative the message may trigger adrenaline. This is particularly so for teenagers. It does repeated damage if we continue to think about it after the event.

For Executives, technology is vital. Deciding you are in control of *it* rather than it controlling *you* though is key. Try to make periods of time when you do not refer to your phone or any other piece of technology. The weekend is an easier time to practice this. Turn it off for short periods or resolve to dump the phone at mealtimes or when you're out walking if you can. Even the connection to it, so that you can listen to music in the gym, can be an issue. Especially if you haven't turned the notifications off!

What is less well known is the relationship between 'checking mode' and addiction. We are designed as creatures of habit, where many of us will repeat a behaviour if it gives us a beneficial 'hit' to do so. Adrenaline can be an addictive substance so the hit we receive can *feel* positive at the time, but it isn't good to have it in your system all the time. This creates over-stimulation and our mind and body can feel under attack. In response, our immune system fires up to protect us, including in our guts and much of the explanation for IBS and other gut complaints can be found in the relationship between stress and events. We all need to take this seriously.

Using the tips earlier in this chapter will help. Sitting and breathing or meditating can trigger the parasympathetic system. This puts you in a better mental and physical state. It is down to us to *decide* to prioritise 'me time' like this and to decide it becomes 'down time' too. Down time is not referring to mood, it's a time when we limit the stimulation we are experiencing. Otherwise, it's a demand. Excessive demands mean we cannot respond without sacrificing our attention to something else. Decide instead to complete a task without distractions. This total focus will increase your productivity.

Total Focus gives us a better chance to feel we have achieved something. Executives can be competitive and like control though. It can be very frustrating to spend a whole day trying to get things done, but feel uncertain of what you've actually achieved!

The Second Principle: E is for Emotional

In 20 years of experience with Executives, I have noticed these two dominant drivers; being *competitive* and liking *control*. Few people I have met find life satisfying without these. Most of the time, these drivers make life interesting. They create a thrill-seeking element to our lives. It *is* possible to thrive on stress *and* these drivers. It comes partly from your attitude *to* something, and our recognition *of it*. If you are not aware of its effects and don't respect your body well enough, then you can become tense. Frustration and anger can be other side effects. These symptoms are the result of a build-up of Cortisol. Cortisol helps us respond to long term exposure to stress. We also need it first thing in the morning when we get out of bed.

Healthy levels of Cortisol are a good thing. When the body feels under attack we need more. Then we undertake something called a 'Cortisol steal'. This is when we prioritise the making of cortisol over our other hormones to keep up with demand. Hormones such as testosterone and oestrogen are vital to our health. If we are to thrive on stress, we *must* find outlets for our emotions or work them out of our body, so that we release them. Otherwise, the demand for cortisol takes priority.

E-motion is energy in motion and negative emotions create negative energy. We feel this all over the body.

The next four tips can help you continue to be competitive or a control freak but also keep you healthy!

1. Sort Dates & Plan to Meet with Friends

In my experience, there are different types of friends. I don't mean some are great and others less so exactly, but that we all need different people to connect with who help us in different ways. Some are ideal for having a drink with, others for your sports activities and still others great to talk to if life is getting you down. If you're lucky enough to have this whole package in one person that can be great, but this is more about making time to connect. Humans are social animals and we need connection (even if we're married), to help us feel close to others.

It can also be an ideal way to dissipate tension if we pick up the phone and organise something regular as a meeting with friends. There can be a balance needed in life as socialising too much can probably leave you pressured to fit it all in, but not having enough down time or just have a change, isn't good for us either. With a bit of planning or making something a regular time in the diary, you can kill two birds with one stone – such as playing squash or tennis.

2. Support and the benefit of a network

For many Executives in senior positions life has occasional, if not frequent, difficulties. This is for a variety of reasons. Many of you thrive on the responsibility and accountability of your role. Other times the role can feel tiring or lonely. This is when connecting with a Mentor, or a group of people, has fantastic benefits for you. That way you're not 'alone' with the issues you experience. If you are a regular member of a group you often receive the benefit of seeing a speaker talk on a topic of interest too. So:

Support Your Brilliance!

The benefits of regular access to other people and their intellectual property are many. They include:

- Building leadership skills

- Problem solving issues you may not have come across before

- Sharing thoughts and ideas

- Learning new skills

- Driving goal setting and planning

- Understanding accounts, balance sheets and margins

The primary reason I am suggesting this, is part of the next recommendation too. When you feel very stressed it can be difficult to feel resilient in the face of the type, or volume, of demands. Having support or someone/ group to connect to can often solve the issue faster. It's important to provide ideas or answers too. We can't know everything all the time, but we tend to set ourselves up as if we expect to!

3. Stabilisers on the Bike

If, and when, life becomes tough I advocate putting stabilisers on your bike. This is when as a child it felt thrilling to learn to ride. It also felt challenging to ride a bike without stabilisers. We all think we prefer this as adults. The problems start though, when we meet a volume of demands, or unforeseen issues. Then we can feel too overwhelmed to master them. This is when we need help. Not input and ideas, but actual physical people who come to help us rather than we who go to them.

Help does not have to mean counselling, and may not even be necessary, but advice is vital! Putting stabilisers on your bike is a metaphor for this type of help. It helps you guide the bike again for a short time until you can take the stabilisers off. There are two stabilisers on a bike, one on the left and one on the right. One might be your family. Take some time and spend it with them. This soothes tension and acknowledges loving, affectionate time with your kids. It can change your mood in the short term, and help you reconnect with the real reason we do what we do in life. Family are often the biggest, and most vital reason we manage businesses. They're also often the reason we try to earn enough to make life positive. This stabiliser works if life is stressful in the short term or in short bursts.

It can be difficult to lean on your family though. Especially when life is becoming *very* demanding. There are different strategies for support when you are *very* stressed. Chronic stress such as this, may feel scary and that's because it lasts longer and gets exhausting. Putting stabilisers on is a shorter-term method and can help to provide a positive answer.

If life is very stressful you might need to reach out to someone who is more knowledgeable than you. This could be a whole group of people. Being honest, direct, and forthright with them may be necessary and valuable. Seeking advice isn't negative. We all feel very keen to achieve and executives feel this particularly. Self-esteem and the fear of failure can prevent someone from reaching out. Asking for input to a situation though *prevents* failure. It isn't a sign *of failure.*

It is also different from being a member of a group and asking for one-off advice. Putting a stabiliser on the bike is asking for an individual, or a group of people to step **in** and help.

When I say this, I am thinking of a client of mine whose business was in a tough retail sector. Through no fault of his own, his primary supplier went bust and my client's business was teetering on the edge. On my advice, he told his wife he needed some time and support. The two of them booked a long weekend together so that they could go walking, and minimise any demands on him. He then got in touch with a group of friends who were all businessman he knew. These friends immediately *parachuted* in. Two of them met with him every week to problem solve what was happening to him. This enabled him to make some critical decisions and think straight. It's a fact of life but a very tough one for an Exec, that you expect yourself to have all the answers. You also expect to make good decisions at a time when you are *most likely* to feel crap yourself. To help you do this you need other people. As a technique this seems to give you the ability to withstand long-term pressures. then the business can stabilise itself - if it's going to. Facing the alternative is vital too. Having a strategy or back-up plan comes from advice too.

Another of his business friends took him out for a beer so that he felt sup-ported but not forced to socialise. A fourth friend had a background in finance and acted as a sounding board whenever needed. He offered options that helped my client problem solve how to borrow money in the short term. He talked about how to downsize his business if that was a better option. In this scenario, I felt as if I did very little, but in my own way I helped guide him so that he stabilized his situation. Hence the term putting stabilisers on your bike!

If you don't know anyone that you would use, I recommend that you look for somebody/people to connect to. Do this whilst life is in a good space and stable, so that they can be there for you when you most need.

4. Spotting the Good Stuff

Life tends to be demanding. We can become very busy, so it can be difficult for us to maintain a positive attitude. It can also be difficult to have a strong sense that things will work out okay.

When life is going well one of the vital strategies you could try might be to use a journal. This is because it helps keep your attitude positive. It can be even more important during stressful times. If you don't like writing much, then a simple daily record last thing at night helps. Think of everything that has gone well that day, or 'one positive thing that mattered today'. List these. It means you will tend to notice, and prioritise, what you have liked. Your mind may be problem-solving, so remembering what you have achieved is important. Life is not all grey, but we filter in the negative.

Many of us are critical of ourselves and others. This might be because we have high standards and if *we* can do it then why can't others? Falling below our own expectations hurts. If we are critical of the outside world, then thinking we are sub-standard isn't acceptable. We begin to feel that laser critique turns on ourselves. This drives our self-talk. Hence the section in the book that describes how to fight back in the face of negativity.

If this behaviour resonates with you, try going back to read the first section. If that isn't enough consider looking at Tony Robbin's work. https:// www. tonyrobbins.com/mind-meaning/how-to-reprogram-your-mind/

He has an excellent approach and I own some of his audio books which I have enjoyed listening to over the years

The Third Principle: P is for Physical

Human beings are complex and everything within our body's interconnects. If you feel tired, sad, or fed up, your emotions will reflect that. Your thoughts influence your physiology too and vice versa. Changing your physiology requires a bit of short-term determination but pays off. Small consistent changes in your habits creates significant change in your biology. That influences how you handle stress.

1. Kicking Sugar

I know I may not be popular saying this, but we are all consuming too much sugar in our diets. Sugar is in a great number of foods and our cooking. The issue is that sugar causes a spike in our blood and insulin has to calm it to reverse the effects. Over-use of this system creates wear and tear. This in turn, reduces efficiency encouraging us to store unwanted fat. We can feel lethargic, and even contributes to diabetes.

Our gut pays a price from this sugar. We still have the guts (stomach, small and large intestine), of our ancestors as we have not changed much. This lack of alteration or adaptation means we are not equipped to cope with a barrage of sugar in our body. The delicate, but important balance of bacteria in the gut imbalance when we eat sugar. Unwanted bacteria begin to thrive instead. Put another way, we get an overpopulation of one type. This prevents the balancing effects of others. Candida is the biggest unwelcome guest in there. Too much sugar creates a trigger for thrush and other unwanted symptoms.

Managing these bacteria is important. Kicking sugar or at least minimising it, will have a very positive effect on your gut. Your mood and your energy levels improve. Many of us misunderstand this and believe that sugar gives us an energy boost. That is because it spikes our blood, but this is very short term. In the medium term, we must cope with that spike. Then blood sugar plummets leaving a nasty drop and a rollercoaster in your day.

TREAT SUGAR WITH RESPECT!

Try swaps instead. Swap dried fruit or natural fruit for sugar in the short term. Try dark chocolate (80% cocoa), to kick your love of the milk stuff. If you can't do this then ease yourself off sugar in all drinks particularly soft drinks and fruit juices. Then reduce it in snacks between meals, and then limit it to a few squares of chocolate AFTER a meal. This will at least minimise the damage.

You will feel surprised at the effects if you minimise sugar in your diet. Take your time doing this as there is no great urgency unless you are diabetic. Limiting your consumption of sugar makes a significant change to health. As you limit it and alter your eating habits your taste buds change. and you will begin to recognise something you've eaten when it has sugar in it. You'll start to taste it again! Then as you gain confidence, it may surprise you to find you *don't want it.* Yes, I know! But it's true. You will not enjoy it as much, as everything with sugar in will taste *too* sweet. Then the benefits will begin to outweigh the downsides of weaning yourself off sugar.

You may lose weight, sleep better and your body will be calmer.

Eat nuts, carrots or veg sticks instead with nut butter or hummus for a snack.

This will pay off in a very short period time.

2. Un-process Your Food

Like sugar, our we bombard our bodies with foods that do not look, or taste, as they would in their natural state. Cooking isn't a problem if you amalgamate foods that look natural before combining them. Processed foods have preservatives in and it is these which cause trouble.

Our cells in our digestive tract act as soldiers would. They patrol all the time. Everything we put in there it treated as a potential threat. Natural, unprocessed foods are much better for us. They do not trigger a problem for our intestine. Being natural foods, they are 'recognised' and broken down. But processed foods trigger an attack from the soldiers. This brings about an immune response and puts our body on alert. Our immune system and digestive tract become inflamed. So does the stomach. Inflammation is a natural reaction, but it triggers a stress response in our body. This releases Cortisol. Chaos can then ensue and all you did was eat!

Protecting your gut means investing in it. It's important to recognise your gut needs regular food. This is best in a simple, natural state, which feeds your brain and body and makes your whole system calm. Here are some examples:

Salmon when cut looks like this:

When cooked, it looks very little different:

Sausage on the other hand is pork or beef that has been squashed and mashed in to a shape, then cooked.

And if you batter it then it's worse! There is a raging debate about fat. I have reviewed the research for years. There is a lot less to worry about if we eat fat with food in its natural state than if we process the food first.

Try to aim for at least one unprocessed meal/ day and eat veg. The recommendation is still 5/day, and these are better if they are vegetables rather than fruit. That's because fruits are sweet. Avoid cereals for this reason unless its porridge. Cook a quick breakfast using eggs, fish or cheese and add simple fruit or veg such as avocado or nuts.

Keep it Simple!

This principle is much better and can create a diverse colony of bacteria. It increases digestion, reduces allergies and improves immune function.

Go for variety in your food. You might want to read Dr Rangan Chatterjee's book on 'The Four Pillars of Health' www.amazon.co.uk. I could have written this book myself such is the similarity in our thinking!

You may also benefit taking a probiotic as these are small, manageable capsules. They contain 5 billion bacteria. There are many strains of bacteria in our gut. Research suggests people who live in the UK may have much less diversity in there. Other, more primitive cultures who do not eat processed food tend to be more diverse. This suggests we are affecting the biodiversity of our gut. We don't know enough about how to ensure the right bacteria are in there. Estimates are between 30 and 400 trillion bacteria within our gut. Supplements may not seem necessary, but you give yourself a good chance of keeping healthy if you do. You also support the immune system. I take Serolife from Serovera. I buy it on www.amazon.co.uk. This tablet has 15 different strains of bacteria. Consult your Dr or a Nutritional Therapist if you are unsure if you should take them though.

3. Keep Hydrated and Drink Water

This one is simple and quick both to write and to do. Water is the best substance for our bodies and the recommendation is to drink about 1 litre/ day. I am surprised at how much better my digestion, general health, skin, and energy levels are when I drink water. It is not that tea and coffee are a mistake, but caffeine is a stimulant. You are already getting a lot of stimulation, both mental and physical. Your lifestyle provides this from work and other sources.

Drinking water helps every cell. Limiting caffeine seems sensible because of its relationship to sleep or lack of it! Many Execs who come in to the practice experience difficulties getting enough sleep. Ensuring quality sleep is vital. Before I write about sleep, a last word on water. Adding fruit for variety can be an easy way to drink a delicious alternative. Flavoured waters might have sugar or sweeteners in them so check the label before you buy.

If you haven't seen one, water bottles with a twistable insert that holds the fruit, are good. This infuses flavour in the surrounding water.

Most sport shops, Lakeland and even Amazon sell these and they are very inexpensive.

4. Sleep and What You Can Do to Encourage It

The biggest benefit of getting enough sleep seems to be how we enable our bodies to repair. Cell renewal and the clearing out of old cells takes place at night. This is Autophagy. Without this vital process we are at risk of creating further stress to our system. Many of us are already under a lot of pressure and hyper-stimulated so we need to invest in 'down time'. We need to put sleep as a matter of priority not as an after-thought. If we make this error then many of us are at risk of increasing internal inflammation. We may become overweight and perform less well. I *know* I make poor decisions and become accident prone when I'm tired. I have recognised the value in investing in my sleep. The return on that investment is as valuable to you as any business you put your hard-earned effort and money in to!

First, aim for a bedtime routine not that unlike one you'd do for your children. They often have a warm bath, some time for a story and then a hug before your child goes off to sleep. As adults we don't do this. We need around an hour or so before bedtime to switch off our phones and avoid all contact with laptops and iPads. If you must look at your phone limit this evening usage to a couple of nights/ week rather than regular habits. This is important if it's something you do such as contacting the U.S. in the evening.

Set your screen to emit less light by checking the settings and altering to a more yellow or amber screen. On an iPhone this is under 'display and brightness'. You can adjust the timings to make sure the yellow light comes on after 9.00pm. This prevents the blue light effect which keeps you awake.

Total darkness is ideal once you go to bed. Reading always seems cosy but use a night light designed to emit more of an amber glow. Philips Sleep & Wake up light available from www.philips.co.uk is around £100 to buy and can do both. It soothes your night time and you wake up better. If you need to get up in the night, a red plug-in night light is ideal. These tend to reduce the shock that comes from turning on a light and are great for babies.

Bright lights shut down melatonin release. We all need melatonin to sleep for lengthy periods otherwise we'll look like this guy….

Blackout curtains are a great as is an eye mask if needed. The main aim is to reproduce a world where there is as little disturbance as possible. This includes electrical buzzing from plug sockets or chargers. Leave those downstairs instead.

A quick word about caffeine as it's important to mention it. Some people do not appear to be sensitive to metabolising caffeine. They report that it makes very little difference to their sleep. If you feel this then you may have become so used to it that your tolerance is high. The rest of us are likely to benefit by modifying our intake especially after midday. Otherwise it takes time to calm back down from drinking it. Having a strong coffee at 6.00pm is likely to still impact our state by midnight. It's no wonder we can find it difficult to slow down well enough to fall asleep. Decaf is not always a good option but it's a great way to start to reduce your intake. If you like flavoured teas chamomile is especially good.

Finally, avoid emotional tension if you can. Keep adrenaline fuelled movies, thrillers, and tough news to earlier in the evening. This includes big chats with your partner. After 9.00pm is risky for your sleep. You'll be more tired at that time and less likely to reach a positive conclusion together. Then the argument can escalate as you score points rather than make a point!

If you are interested in reading more tips on sleep, please visit my site www.suefirthltd.com. Here you'll find the Useful Links page.

You can find comprehensive information about sleep here: http://yoohealth.com/sleep-deprivation-causes-symptoms-and-treatment/.

The Fourth Principle: S is for Self

Time for ourselves is often a luxury for an Executive. Work pressures, family, and young children influence how much time we have. Often the need to achieve and control affect this too. Some struggle to generate down time as they 'push' at life to achieve. Many Executives are competitive and perfectionist. This can create conflicting drives within them. They strive to achieve a great deal but never know when they get there!

Coming to terms with this or making 'peace' with yourself can be helpful. Rather than 'fighting' this need within you, move *towards* it, and play to your strengths. If you are competitive, like to achieve big things, or use adrenaline as jet fuel, then do so with a purpose. This time its with the purpose of enjoying yourself!

1. Have a Hobby or 2!

Hobbies are both 'down time' and 'me time'. Aim for a complete change. Look for those that are enjoyable and alter your 'state' for the better. I always suggest you think about one hobby that is an adrenaline fuelled. These include racing, football and team sports in general. Then contrast that with a softer, calmer, more creative hobby. Examples include meditation, mindfulness and being still but creative hobbies are vital too.

Examples of calming or creative hobbies to think about are:

- Walking

- Hiking in nature

- Camping

- Cooking

- Yoga/Pilates

- Fun with your kids such as helping them draw, make a model, or write something

- Keeping a journal

- DIY (at times as long as you're patient!)

- Learning new things by attending a class

- Reading

- Gardening

- Board games

- Audio books

- Singing or joining a group or choir

- Playing music or playing an instrument

- Photography

- Fishing

- And there are lots more………………!

Hobbies are an easy way to achieve complete focus and do something you enjoy. Exercise such as running, weight training or playing squash also dissipates adrenaline.

2. Plan Regular Breaks and Holidays

Holidays fit in to two types of solution for stress. The first, is what I call a 'reboot'. This has the capacity to make you feel better because it takes you away from typical situations. It gives you a change and a rest. A short break such as a long weekend is ideal for this. If you can, go on a Friday and come back on the Monday or Saturday to Tuesday could work too.

Re-boots are a specific way to get away but not for long. You may wish to restrict the use of your mobile phone or the frequency with which your workplace can get hold of you. Resist the temptation to keep checking your phone. You can do this by reducing the frequency of notifications you receive. Plan some fun and easy ways to chill out instead. Plan several of these short weekend breaks every year as this gives you something to look forward to.

The second type is the more typical. A proper holiday which will include family. Holidays are important. They give you an opportunity to reconnect with essential people in your life. Our families are crucial to us so get them involved in planning the holiday. Holidays are also different from a reboot. I have always described the life of an Executive as needing time in thirds. You were a person before you married, and before you had children, so if it's relevant, aim to find time to do all 3.

1/3 on your own

1/3 with your husband or wife/ partner

1/3 with your family

3. Hugs and Affection

Here I am talking about giving or receiving a hug and being affectionate. Humans are social animals and we thrive on touch. This released Oxytocin. It can be nice to give a hug to someone and definitely to receive one. This is easier in your personal life than it is at work. Hugs and hugging are a quick way to dissipate tension and feel better.

At times it will not be possible to do this, or you may not feel like it. Deep emotional tension increases our cortisol production. This sends the message to the body to feel under attack. In this state we are more likely to feel very wired or anxious. Reaching out to hug someone or ask for a hug may seem much less appealing.

When you feel like this there can be a great deal of value in going for a sports massage. Cortisol leaves hard, grisly knots in our muscles which in turn feel sore. Massage pushes these knots around and breaks them down. It eases how tight the muscle feels and how tired you can feel as a result.

If you have time you may want to have a bath in the evening. This is best done when you can sit in a deep bath for up to 20 minutes with some Epsom Salts in the water. Epsom salts are Magnesium Sulphate. They are the fastest way to dissipate Cortisol and aches in the muscle. Put a large handful in the water and allow it to work by 'taking up' magnesium through your skin. You can buy Epsom Salts at large branches of a chemist or online through Amazon. Westlab themselves sell it or this link: www.epsomsalts.co.uk.

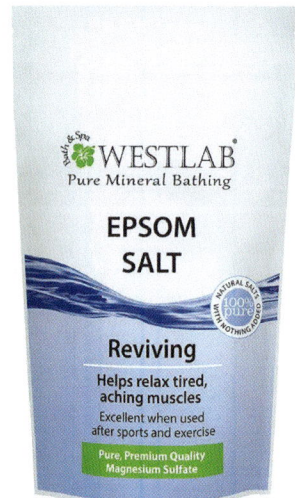

WESTLAB
Pure Mineral Bathing

EPSOM SALT

100% pure
NATURAL SALT WITH NOTHING ADDED

Reviving

Helps relax tired, aching muscles
Excellent when used after sports and exercise

Pure, Premium Quality
Magnesium Sulfate

4. Variety and Change

I've spent most of this chapter emphasising how much stimulation Executives experience. It is important to reduce this over-activity at certain times of the day and in your lives in general. Executives can find lack of activity boring. They can feel as stressed by this as others would be with constant movement!

If you know you like keeping active and find it difficult to relax, then try to 'rest' in the day. Put in place a series of 'pit stops'. These give you variety so wherever you can, pause for 10 to 15 minutes. Take a walk in the daylight for that period of time, or change the pace and surf the net for a bit. Try to stop, pause, and breathe (5-2-5).

Variety is the Spice of Life!

You are not a Maclaren car though. It's not in your interests to undergo a pit stop within the recent world record of 1.92 seconds! Felipe Masse completed this with his Williams racing team. Your aim is to take your time rather than be against the clock. Sit with a coffee near the window for the light, the view, and to pause, or read a book for a bit. Watch your favourite video of your kids on your phone. Look at some of your best photos on your desk (computer if you must) and let yourself press 'pause'.

In conclusion: we are all using adrenaline every day, but Executives try to live on it. We can thrive on stress but only if we respect what it's doing to our bodies and change our lifestyles to cope. If you want 'sustainable performance' this is the only way to do it.

4 When Life Gets Tough! Steps 1 to 4

If like me, you are an impatient person, then you will desire to find solutions to your situation. In my experience, many Executives know *what they need* but not *how* to get it. They want to feel better but are not always sure how to achieve this. That's because it's rare they get in to a situation they feel they cannot handle, or at least try to alter. As a result, they often persevere for long periods of time. This drains them, their adrenals and their passion for life. In general, they dislike feeling confused. Instead, they prefer knowing what to do and how to do it. But living in a state where they feel uncertain, unhappy, or unsettled, can feel out of control. Lacking a sense of personal control is one of the biggest causes of stress for an Executive. Much of the time life is within their influence, especially if they run their own business.

When an Exec comes through my door in central London, they've reached a personal 'low'. I find a pragmatic approach to be best. Other coaching or counselling models tend to take an hour at a time and use a process that acts like a 'pull me' model. The counsellor *pulls* information out of people, then pulls the solutions too. This is so that *the client* thinks of them, rather than telling the individual what to do. I know there are strong reasons why they do this. If you've ever watched Meryl Streep in the film 'It's Complicated' you will smile when you watch how she door-steps her counsellor. She pleads with him to tell her what to do after having rekindling a relationship with her ex-husband. This was after 10 years of living without him. You can almost *feel* her frustration as she leaves, reciting his words "you must do what you think is best". How is she supposed to do that when she doesn't know?

Why go to see someone if you get told to come up with your own solutions! I grew tired of this model and instead designed one of my own. I see people for 2 hours at a time, sometimes 3 hours and never less. To do justice to their issue/s it's important to take time. To get them to a better head space, it's important to do it well. The only way to do that, is to tell them what to do and to set goals (which appeals to their focussed nature). Then hold them accountable (which also appeals to their drive).

I find there is instant peace in making a plan to find the answers. Most Executives I meet spend a great deal of time focussed on getting from A to C in life. They have a strategy for getting from A to C. But when something steers the ship off course and they can't do it the way they want to, they get stressed. They continue to use the same impatient rules they adopt for everything in life. So why not appeal to this drive? I get them from A to C in the shortest possible time and it pays off. They feel better because they know what to do; they are back in control and can call the shots. Trauma isn't the same. It needs a different kind of management. But general situations respond well. In the following pages I now bring that strategy to you.

Step 1: Lay the Problems Out on Paper

My recommendation is that things are a lot easier to see and deal with when they are out of your head and down on paper. It's easier to make choices and to rationalise what is contributing to the stress. The best place to start is with several pages of A4 paper. Then write down the issue/s as you know them. Spread them about like this:

Keep writing the issues until you have it all down on the paper. Then start with the next problem in a similar format, laying it all out. There is a genuine benefit in doing this. You cannot get exhausted from going over and over the problems now that you are writing them down. We know the psychological benefit in getting something out of your head and sorting it.

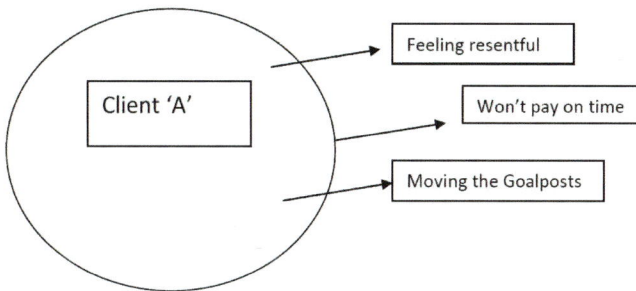

Next comes a simple principle of walking away for a while. Take a bit of time out and do something else for a few hours then come back to the issues as you've laid them out. Now ask yourself 3 questions:

- What have I tried to do about each of these dilemmas?

- What else can do to resolve them? Include help from others here and if so, who? Write down anything that fixes it or begins to, even if it's 'blue sky' or unlikely to happen

- Then ask yourself, what is the *one thing* that if I were to do it, would begin to bring about an improvement in this problem?

Write your answers down. If it helps discuss the issue with a friend, colleague or expert. **Action is without doubt the best solution to stress especially for an Executive.** Small steps help you to focus. Small steps turn into cumulative change. Things you *can* do rather than every possible reason not to be able to move forward on it.

Step 2: Reach Out

When someone comes to see me, they are often 'pretending' everything is ok. It's not that they mean to do this, but many of us hate being vulnerable. Admitting to a problem is a form of vulnerability few of us cope well with. To admit there is an issue can be painful. What I mean by 'reaching out' isn't always to an expert like myself, it's to the people that matter to you too. In other words, consider if you are presenting a fake or artificial 'front' to your friends and loved ones. It might be in order not to upset them. Many of us do this as parents to protect our children from seeing how we are struggling with something. Whilst I accept this can be appropriate for children of a young age, it doesn't help older kids/ adults or a partner. That's because they don't know that something is wrong.

When we decide to show our closest loved ones that we need support for a bit there can be a breakthrough. It can be uncomfortable to do this. Many of us think we are the *rock* in a relationship and this discloses we are unhappy or struggling. But you often gain from this level of honesty and it gives your family a chance to rally round. Other people cannot help if they don't know you need it. Your defence mechanism is like a coat. This is one that you choose to take off in the warmth of close family. It's also one you can also choose to *put back on* when needed.

I am not advocating you feel the need to remove this coat when you are with business colleagues. I know this can send the wrong message as employees may feel nervous or jump to the wrong conclusions. Letting family know things are not quite right in your world and you need some time, can help though. It buys you the space and opportunity to sort it.

If you don't like the idea of this then consider it a 'straight conversation'. Have this with yourself, and *then* with your family. Most Executives I know respond well to being direct – not unkind or brash, but straight. So, start with having a straight conversation with yourself. Give yourself a few minutes 'talking to'. For example, say to yourself, "I gain nothing if I keep pretending everything is fine. My wife/ husband/ close friend/s can't help me if I don't talk to them". Talking is healthy and might even be helpful. Sit each one of them down and help them understand what's happening with you right now they can try to help. That way you at least buy yourself time and the *right* people start to come to the fore.

Find the right time and choose the right place to sit down with them. Have a glass of wine, and be natural about it but the rules are as follows: be gentle, be truthful and be honest. You are aiming to be transparent so that they know you are in pain or need time. Tell them this is why you might be grumpy or withdrawn.

If you're reluctant to do this then recognise it's not about disclosing too much (should you feel that is best). It's about aiming for greater openness so that you are not being stoic at this stage of your life or all the time. You can't have your act together all the time. This does not give you permission to go through a tough phase in your life. We all need help sometimes. I once saw this saying and loved it!

Honesty is better than sugar-coated Bullshit!

When there is an opportunity to talk to your loved ones it shows you value them and that you *choose* to talk to them. This helps to build trust rather than detracting from it.

Then consider the following tip...

Step 3: Ask for Support

When you talk to your closest friends or relations like this, have a goal in mind. What I mean is something you feel *they can do for you*. Even if all you ask for is time to sort the issues, you are asking for understanding. Other ideas include to ask them if they might sort their own problems for a bit. This is so that you can be free to concentrate on what *you* need. This is especially useful if they are grown up kids, as they've got used to leaning on you for all the answers. It can be very tiring to be the problem solver in the family, the fixer, and the solution-giver. It 'sets you up' to have all the answers but doesn't often enable you to have 'needs' of your own.

It's also important to remember:

You don't have to have it all
figured out to move forward!

If you have a problem with your business, the strategy is much the same. This time you need a variety of people to support you. I have been both a member and a speaker of organisations for business in the past. Options include Vistage and The Advisory Board or TAB as well as Footdown. These are organisations you pay to join. You meet monthly with a group of like-minded professional people. They run businesses of their own, and can relate to many of the experiences you have too. One of the most valuable assets of being a member of a group like this is the phenomenal resource they offer. Someone in your group is very likely to have experienced what you're going through. The Chair for your group has the prerogative of offering a 1:1 meeting too. This provides a confidential sounding board.

This is the same as 'putting stabilizers on your bike'. I referred to this in the previous chapter.

Here is an example: a client of mine (let's call him John), was having a hard time at work. He ran the business and had grown it with his brother to a considerable size. The problem though, wasn't in the business but lay with John. He wasn't happy and after some years of struggling he finally reached out to me. With my help he was able to see the role wasn't right for him and he was *trying to be something he wasn't.* He was very capable, loved sales and the ambassadorial side of his work. He didn't enjoy running the

business and the day to day decision making or the accountability. He was also compared to his brother who found all these things much easier. When John realised this, we had a direction to take his problem solving and action planning. The stabilizers on the bike, were his family who he asked for support whilst he took some time out for a few weeks. I was the other stabilizer. His brother had to support the leadership gap that resulted after John was absent for a bit. He was happy to do this though as it was his skill anyway. They worked out how to buy John out of his half of the business. Then discussed how to run the amalgamated businesses and decided to put in a new M.D.

It's a Question of Confidence

It's an assumption that top Executives have all the answers all the time. If that's the expectation you have, then that puts a lot of pressure on you. We do this not only about *what* to do but also feel we can't experience uncertainty or doubt. Self-doubt is a normal human emotion. An Executive who is experiencing uncertainty, can feel a failure and this fear can deepen. Fears like this plague a troubled Executive even when there is no evidence to support this. It becomes second nature to feel a lacking of confidence. You can talk yourself into a very anxious state without seeing much proof or real sign of actual failure.

The mere *anticipation* of failure keeps them up at night and fuels nightmares. To combat this, it is critical to focus on what you *can do* to influence the situation. If this is not actually controlling a situation, stay focussed on your action plan. Getting help to know what action to take can be important. Bouncing ideas around with others builds conviction. It builds confidence, and regains a sense of personal control.

All the Executives I have met feel better once they begin to feel in control of a difficult situation. This is because they *need* control in their lives. They are at their best when they have that level of autonomy. They thrive under more stress than most others would desire. But that position or place in life, for an Executive, *is living!* Anything less, is boring and lacks the thrill.

Consider this:

> When you can't control what's happening,
> challenge yourself to control the way
> you respond to what's happening.
> That's what matters!

Step 4: Me Time

Having a few moments to yourself every day is vital for easing strain when you are deeply stressed. Our minds are a problem solving, goal seeking mechanism. They can focus on a habitual thought or issue even (if it is a negative thought), and this changes your chemistry. Only when YOU decide to stop it and tell your brain to concentrate on something else, will this change. We have a powerful mechanism going on in there, it's clever and will pursue any goal you set it. A negative thought is also a goal. Anxieties, personal fears and self-doubt become something to think about. But worrying about something doesn't change it. Only action alters the stress. The critical thing is to recognise this. It isn't *your fault,* but it is *a fault* of the system that we develop a profound difficulty in shutting the process down! Many people I meet say they cannot relax or stop thinking about work or their troubles. This is due to the problem-solving nature of our thinking. Changing this only happens once the situation changes. This is why you have to keep busy DOING something to resolve it. Occupy your mind with thoughts of action and planning solutions. OR keep it busy thinking about other things by doing something else that needs focus. You have to force it to take a rest from the problem at hand. For example, doing an exercise class means you CAN-NOT think about the work issue at that time.

This is the best reason to exercise. Even more important than the idea that it helps keep us fit because many of us are sedentary. Exercise shifts cortisol in your muscles and may release DHEA. You can often feel better even if only for a short time. This is because it dissipates tension. Taking part in activities you *want* to do is helpful. Your main aim is to stay focussed and preoccupied. The trouble is, many of us do not feel sociable when stressed. If you can push yourself a little to make it out for a drink, go for supper somewhere, go for a run or go to the gym it's better. It will help you feel good.

The other reason exercise is important is because of something called 'dual processing'. Your brain cannot pay equal attention to two things at once. This is a feature of everyone's mind. So, it's best to plan something that requires complete focus. You CANNOT concentrate on your thoughts to the same degree. Focussed exercise requires you to listen. Whilst you are listening to someone else you cannot listen to your own thoughts! Taking a class or lesson in canoeing, surfing or yoga are good examples when you're stressed. The aim isn't to become competitive, or perfectionist, it's to keep busy! If you're going to go for a run for example, you could go with someone for the short term. This would be better than going alone for now. You may even be able to chat!

Psychologists and therapists use this rule of dual processing in their favour. We encourage a client to concentrate on a moving object and talk to them at the same time. If you watch someone's finger move back and forth as in the therapy of an EMDR* session you cannot get anxious. This enables the therapist to help emotions and distress about a traumatic event. You cannot get anxious whilst paying attention to movement. I have found this to be a brilliant and very gentle way to help people. Psychologists treat soldiers returning from combat who suffer from post-traumatic stress this way. It's also good for people whose life has taken a traumatic, or dramatic, turn. You can find an EMDR practitioner by looking on the website listed at the back of the book.

Conclusions

Taking 'time out' or time to yourself is essential to help you cope well, even if only for short periods of time. Some people sit on a rocker and drink a cup of tea/ coffee early in the morning before the household wakes up. Others use their hobbies to break up the day, and still others use exercise and friends as I've recommended here

We can become withdrawn otherwise, so talking, smiling and being sociable need effort. It is good to avoid isolation.

When Life Gets Tough! Steps 5 to 10

Step 5: Heal the Past

Our past experiences are a vast resource of information. Our brains use this information much as we would search for answers using Google on the internet. We type in a question and ask for input or solutions when we're on our computers. Your brain works much the same way. If you ask it something specific then the same kind of search and filter mechanism goes in to motion. Everything you have been through is in your memory.

It is important to know that this happens with both positive and negative events. They are *equally* fast using the search and identify facility. But the problem is when we have too many negative events in our past or those same events are VERY traumatic. Your memory will attempt to recover them to help you AVOID them. Funny, isn't it? You have a built-in ability to avoid repeating mistakes. Yet the very technique it employs, helps you by repeatedly reminding you of the mistake!

The point is, we may not be able to go back and change the events, but it can pay off to change your thoughts *about the event*. Tackling, revisiting, and modifying what you have been through pays off. This is because it reduces the significance or importance of the event in your mind. It minimises the frequency it revisits it. If you reduce how often it recalls, then you will not be as troubled by it. Imagine these events to be rather like flags, I call them 'red flags' which pop up when you look back. If you have a lot of red flags that wave at you every time you think back on your life, then you could feel inadequate. You'll remind yourself of your weaknesses, or reasons to doubt yourself. This isn't a recipe for feeling good!

Pain is a physical and emotional tension. It drains you and takes vital energy from your daily life. It's important to recognise this. Someone else's opinion of you can become a red flag. Every time you look back you think about this. But that is *their* opinion. It isn't yours. It you *believe it* then it becomes yours and weighs heavy. Becoming lighter is important. If you were overweight, you'd eat less, or exercise more. The same needs to happen in your mind and memories. Past painful memories become heavy and drain you. Many of us do not realise this and don't choose to work on it. If being an ideal weight is good for us why not an ideal mind?

Re-visiting events to scrutinize and review them is important for two reasons. First, we need to learn the lessons the event/s taught us. Second, we need to question how valuable the memory is and dump it! Reviewing them makes them smaller. It stops the red flag effect, or to use a computer metaphor, it has the effect of minimizing the screen. This makes it *optional* to enlarge it again and your mind minimizes the stress with it

So, how do you do this?

One way is to write letters. You may have heard of this before as a psychological technique. If you haven't heard of it you may want to give it a try.

A client of mine (let's call him Dave), was an Executive who approached me several years ago. His trouble was a low opinion of himself. He hid it well when at work. He ran a business of approximately 50 people and it was family owned. But he felt significant self-doubt. When we scrutinized this, we found these doubts came from the way his father had treated him. Dave's father wasn't a very affectionate man. He'd corrected his son by both criticising his choices, behaviour, and ideas. He also employed something I called 'silent disagreement'. That is the kind of look that showed he didn't like something, but he didn't say it. The effect was the same, and it 'wired' Dave to walk on eggshells. This affected him. He changed how he expressed things to his father. He also feared the reaction or disapproval of other people.

Such was his difficulty, Dave felt a slow shyness creep in to his life. It was easier not to proffer an opinion or try to discuss anything than to risk getting disapproved of. It saddened me to hear this because of the damage it had done. It had affected Dave in his teenage years whilst his father was still alive. For 20 years since his father's death Dave had remained uncertain. There was a secondary impact in that some of Dave's employees from when his father ran it were still in the business. Dave felt burdened by what he *thought* was their silent disapproval. The important point was that he never actually *heard* them say anything but he believed it.

This kind of perceived disapproval isn't imagined. It can be *amplified* by your own thoughts though. This is relevant because Dave can't change the way he thinks about events in the past, but he *can* change how he feels now. He can't speak to his father, but in my experience, there is merit in talking to him *as if he could.* The best way to do that seems to be through the written word.

I advised Dave to write to his father. In a letter of this type you have total freedom to write whatever you want. There are no rules so there is no need, or point, in feeling guilty for saying something unkind or harsh. You wouldn't say this in person but in the letter you can say what you like. Even if the individual you may want to write to is still alive, this is a letter that you will **never** send. It is for your purposes to bring *you* relief

Where do you start?

Start anywhere in time but I would suggest you take a red flag event, and begin there. Begin to describe this. For example write down "when we were travelling to 'x' and you and mum had an argument in the car you shouted at her. Itt made me feel…………."

This doesn't have to be a logical, sensible download. Begin anywhere in time and go from there. As you write, describe the event until you have said everything you think is relevant. Then follow that up with your emotions. Write about them and how the event affected you then, and how it affects you now. If you're angry tell him or her. Let the anger out first then direct your thoughts towards any pain or hurt you feel. Write about that too

For example, if you felt disappointed, upset, lonely, abandoned or hurt, write about it. Ask them questions, "how could you?" or "why did you let this happen?" whatever it is, let it out on paper. This is a 'safe' medium, say what you feel and above all keep writing until you begin to feel relief.

It is less important that they can/ cannot answer than the fact that you let it out. When you have taken your time – revisiting it over several days if you need to – stop. My genuine advice is that unlike a letter you would send, do not re-read this for grammatical mistakes. You are not judged by whether this is well written. Give yourself permission to say the things you may *never* have said, or ever will say, aloud.

At the end of the letter stop, fold it, and leave it alone for a day or two. When you are ready read it ONE LAST TIME then you need to decide about what to do with it. One of three possible options exist here. Either a) accept this happened, you don't have to like it, but accept it let it go now. Or, b) I have learnt from this (then write about what you have learnt), or c) I forgive you for this. The last option is very personal and *your* choice. No-one will judge if you cannot choose the last option but the previous 2 are ok and will suffice. Decide which one you believe you are ready to do. Then sign the letter as you would with your signature.

Now you have 2 further options: either keep it in a very safe place in a box in the loft and resolve not to look at it again. Or the second option is you burn it.

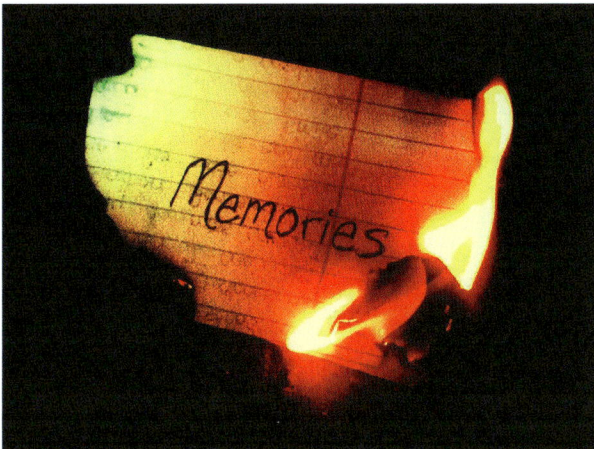

The latter is when you desire total closure. The sadness, anger or hurt within the pages is something you no longer want. Go to a quiet place and put the letter in a safe environment – such as a burner for a BBQ and set fire to it. Watch it until it goes out and say a quiet statement meant to release it. Let the pain go, and say goodbye. In my experience, the emotional relief you feel is profound. You can write to anyone this way. Relatives, clients, and significant people in your past. Anyone who has done you real harm. Write until the pain eases.

For profound trauma such as abuse, writing alone is unlikely to be enough. I urge you to look for a reputable therapist who practices support for trauma. An EMDR (eye movement desensitisation and reprocessing), expert who can help you. There is information about this at the back of the book.

Once Dave wrote his letter, he took it a place his father often went. He said a few quiet words. He asked that his father understood he was not the same man as him. He was a *different* man with different methods and he was *not* going to judge himself anymore.

Step 6: Focus on the Positive in the Past

Writing letters this way reduces the impact negative events can have. It then becomes important to value the positive events you've been through. For example, succeeding at things helps you know that you *can* succeed. It gives you the confidence to try new things.

I call these events 'green flags. My aim is to get you to look back on your life and highlight the positive events. These act as signposts so that they see examples of how well you have done in your life.

The way to begin is to complete an exercise called 'The Lifeline Exercise'. Take a large piece of paper, preferably A4 or bigger and draw a horizontal line from left to right in the middle of the page. Starting with 0 on the left which represents the day you were born and ending with your age now on the right, place little lines to represent your age split in 10-year gaps like this:

0	10	20	30	40	50+

Above and below the line write as much information as you can. Think about the events you experienced in each period. So, between the ages of 10 and 20 you might have learnt to drive or pass exams. Between the ages of 20 and 30 you might have married, or had children. You could have passed your degree. Keep thinking and writing until there are several events in each section. Pay attention to recent years. Work backwards in case you cannot remember much about the years between 0 and 10.

For each event, list your characteristics. What did it take to do the things you have written about on this page? For example, what did it need to pass your driving test? It may have taken persistence, determination, and confidence.

To get married it may have taken courage, love, and dedication. To pass a degree it may have taken intelligence. To get your first promotion, you may be professional, credible and knowledgeable. Keep writing a list of the characteristics until you have lots of them. Then take a third page and flesh out your list of strengths like this:

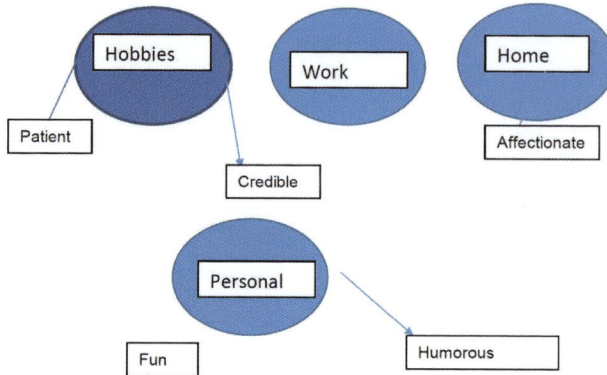

Your main aim is to look at yourself in all these different contexts and think about what you can be like. Your Lifeline exercise may have given you lots of ideas. But you may not have remembered everything. Your hobbies for example, or how you can be with your family. List these different situations and think about them too. In other situations, you may be capable, intuitive, or decisive. By the end of this part of the exercise though, you should have a decent list of your strengths. Then if you wish, you can re-write these on a small card to carry this around.

Some people may value being able to look at the list when they are feeling low. For example, if you're frustrated or if something isn't going well or you've had a tough day. Others will prefer to keep it on a computer and access it when they are home. Either way, let the list act as a reminder that you are very capable. You have done well at different things over the years.

If you need to, remind yourself of these daily. Share them with others in an appropriate way. For example "I never realised I could be a persistent person until…….." or, "it's easy to believe I'm not clever but when I took my exams I found.........". Listen to yourself when you're talking and refer to your strengths in conversation. Try very hard not to put yourself down. Instead of "that's typical of me", say something positive such as "I can achieve things when I try".

Step 7: Change the Way You Are Thinking, Use a Therapist If Needed

This next tip is to encourage you to tackle the way you think. This is because some people can find themselves sliding towards depression. It can be very difficult for someone. It's particularly difficult for an Executive because they can feel very uncomfortable. Your ability to stay on top of life is very important to you. Depression can feel as if you're not on top of things anymore.

The symptoms of depression are quite specific:

A consistent and persistent sense of sadness or even despair. This is a chemical shift and can result in a loss of focus, concentration, and memory. It tends to feel as if you're thinking through a fog and this becomes difficult to clear. In my experience people who go to the Dr and ask for medication can feel a significant improvement in mood. This isn't necessarily the right thing for everyone. The lifestyle changes I've listed in the previous chapter can be enough. Give yourself a chance to do what you can to ease these feelings. They may be short lived *and* you get to learn a toolkit to correct life. If you do not feel better after several weeks though, please consider going to see your doctor.

One of the issues is that a person must *desire* to get better. Only that way can you decide to 'fight back'. It requires a *determined effort* to overcome depression. If that's how you're feeling please stop pretending everything's ok. There will be significant people who need to support you. Reach out and tackle the things that need altering in bite size steps. Put all personal long-term plans on hold for a bit, so that you are not overwhelmed, daunted or anxious. Stick to very short deadlines so that you can see results and *feel* things coming back in to your control.

Case Study

A couple of years ago an Executive I met felt shocked at how terrible he felt. He couldn't get himself out of bed, had no desire to work and **no** idea what to concentrate on to get the work done. His business was not in trouble, but he had slipped in to a very low state.

Sliding down towards depression is very unpleasant. He felt dispirited because he *couldn't* get back up by himself. A member of Vistage was a friend and had heard me speak in the past. He contacted me and asked for my help. The first thing I did was ask the friend to rally the other members of the group. Their aim was to help decide who was the most capable employee in the business. They asked that employee to step up as interim Director which put someone in charge. This gave the Chief Executive the time to work on his unhappiness. It also stopped the fear that the business would suffer because no-one was at the helm.

I then recommended that the same friends take it in turns to visit, call, or pay attention to his business. This was best done weekly until the Director had built his confidence to manage the business. It would have the added benefit of enabling the friends to stay in touch with the profit and loss of the company. They would be visiting the absent Chief Exec and could fill him in with how things were.

TAKING THE STRESS OUT OF LEADERSHIP

The Chief Executive came to me, talked and I listened. There was nothing I could *hear* that told me why he was unhappy. He had drifted to a place and he couldn't navigate his way out. Although I put in place the practical steps above, and talked to his wife, he deteriorated further. The problem is that I am **not** with someone all the time. In those moments when they are on their own, they have a *lot of time* to think. Thinking is not always a good thing. The *way* we think and what *we think about* is key to our recovery. It can also make us drift downwards. He began to despair that he needed to take time off and that the business would fail. Although there was **no evidence** that this was happening, he couldn't stop worrying about it. He stopped getting in touch and after I contacted him again, I heard nothing for a couple of weeks. Concerned, I rang and learned that he had experienced a particularly anxious weekend. This had resulted in a breakdown and his wife had called his doctor.

They took him to a psychiatric ward where his treatment helped him recover some weeks later. This was sad for me and very difficult for him. Sometimes stress turns to depression and depression to despair. This is sometimes at a speed that we cannot foresee. It is then that you'll need a therapist or psychiatrist to help. It is rare though, but your loved ones will help you recognise when this has happened. For mild depression you must *desire* to get better and from there you begin to fight back!

Step 8: Start Acting!

I've already mentioned that our thinking becomes faulty. These thoughts need 'breaking down' to alter the way we view things. To be fair, it is much easier to do this with external support. External support is objective and can bring some tools to the discussions that help. One such tool is Cognitive Behavioural Therapy. At the end of the book I recommend titles to read to do some CBT for yourself. In general, I would suggest you find a reputable therapist to help you identify what to tackle. They can tell you how and then hold you accountable or encourage you to apply the tools. With consistent effort you target small changes for yourself. You can alter what I call the 'touch points' or times when you are most likely to allow faulty thinking to take hold. Each one of these moments is an opportunity to change your thinking. This alters your chemistry for the better and makes a difference over time.

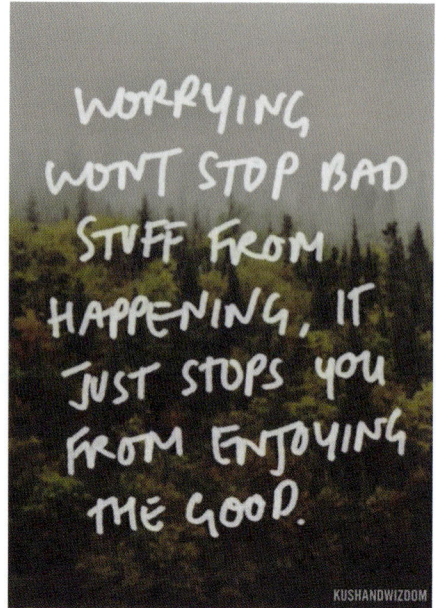

WORRYING WONT STOP BAD STUFF FROM HAPPENING, IT JUST STOPS YOU FROM ENJOYING THE GOOD.

KUSHANDWIZDOM

To Recap

The key is **focus** and **action**! We get overwhelmed when we face too much at once. Stress makes a marked difference to this. It exacerbates our fear that we are not managing and that we will fail. The *only* solution to is to shorten the timescales. Reduce the size of the goal, and put the odds in your favour by starting to achieve results. The best results are bite size victories. Small victories are indicative of you fighting back and things begin to improve. As they improve, your confidence builds. It might take time to achieve what you need but bite size chunks and rewards keep you motivated. If you need, keep a daily list of what you've achieved that day, rather than a list of *what you still need to do*. This has the added benefit of helping you stay in touch with how far you've come.

Step 9 and 10: Keep in Mind What You Can Influence & Keep ACTING!

This should have the effect of helping you feel more in control. But people can slip or have a setback which magnifies due to their stress. Re-visit the previous steps and start again. If you need reach out for support and keep focussed on what you want to do or the plans you've made. Wherever necessary seek therapeutic help to ease this struggle.

I sometimes find it can help to keep a diary or journal during this stage. It gives you an outlet for your frustrations, and keeps track of progress. It could also record your triggers for anger, frustration, and strong negative emotions.

To Recap: The Steps

Top Ten Tips for Stress!

- **Lay the problems out & begin making decisions:** write them down, identify related themes & keep going until everything is on the table
- **Reach out:** other people cannot help unless they can 'see' that you need it. Try to stop being stoic & show them the real person
- **Ask for support:** anyone who is important to you needs to know you are overwhelmed so let them know what you need
- **Me Time:** think about taking little bits of time to yourself every day in order to recover, exercise and relax
- **Heal the Past:** pain is a physical & emotional tension. It drains us, taking vital energy and preoccupying our thoughts
- **Focus on the positive in the past:** identify situations where you have coped by completing the Lifeline Exercise. Pull out your strengths and remind yourself daily
- **Change your thinking to tackle negative thoughts:** use the CBT work we do to help remind you to 'fight back!'
- **Focus on the future & what you want:** decide what you want to change, take bite size chunks and take steps to do it, rewarding yourself as you go.
- **Then begin concentrating on the positive in your daily life:** remind yourself to emphasise how far you've come, what you *can* influence or change & what there is to be grateful for
- **Review your progress:** continue to tackle each problem, taking action, recognising your achievements and keeping a journal or diary if it appeals

The next chapter helps deepen your knowledge. Only by analysing *who or what* is adding to your stress can you identify how you tackle it. Otherwise we all tend to blame ourselves. In the next chapter I help you achieve a better perspective.

5 The Difference Between Sources and Causes of Stress

This chapter deepens your knowledge about stress. This is so that you can differentiate between *what* is stressing you, and *why* it is an issue for you. There is a difference between external triggers of stress. These are sources of stress and 'causes' of stress which are within us.

To explain, a source of stress is any experience that triggers stress in us. To define it:

An external event, situation, or person.

What we mean by external is outside of us. So, it is something that happens to us. We then think about it. Everyone thinks about everything they experience. In fact, it's not *what* happens to us but our thoughts about it that matters. The stress response is automatic. But how much stress we experience after the event is due to our thoughts about it.

In general, an event is a one-off experience. It can be significant and intense, but it can also be something we recover from. A 'situation' results from multiple events that create cumulative stress. For example, losing a client is an event. Then experiencing cash flow difficulties makes the situation worse. This might be the cumulative impact of a situation. Another example is being made redundant. This is an event the day it happens, but *living with the effect of redundancy* is a situation. The important point is to watch for the significant impact that person, event, or situation *has on you*.

The Health & Safety Executive have identified there are 6 common sources of stress at work. These are very similar to what I have said: the number of demands, the amount of support you have, how much control you have in your role, the relationships at work, the nature of the role and how much change you experience. You can find more information on these here: http://www.hse.gov.uk/stress/standards/

These are 'sources' of stress. It's the individual themselves who determines how these situations trigger stress within them.

In the previous chapter I suggested you write down the issues that were troubling you. This was step 1, to lay the problems out on paper. Here is a list of typical sources of stress in everyday life:

Example Sources of Stress

Christmas	Difficult people
Work	Children
Change	Computers
Traffic jams	Retirement
Presentations	Redundancy
Being late	My Boss
Deadlines	Learning something new

The difficulty with sources of stress is that they can be very broad. So, the next step is to be as **specific** as possible about each source. For example, if you wrote that your client was the source, what is it about your client that is the problem? If change is an issue, then be specific about what happens or troubles you in relation to change.

It is very important to work out *what* the issue is. Think about what or who, it is that gives you anxiety. Now determine how bad your stress is. This is like the questions you had to ask yourself when identifying your symptoms. You are determining the frequency, intensity, and duration of your sources of stress.

Ask yourself on a scale of 1 to 10: How often do you experience this? How bad (intense), do you feel about it? We all experience troublesome issues, but we do not feel the need to tackle *all* of them.

To have the motivation to change something it would have to bother you a lot.

Next, check out how motivated you are to change? Can you change yourself, your lifestyle, or the situation for the better? The best change is really the one that starts with your attitude.

Ask yourself on a scale of 1 to 10 how willing are you to tackle this issue? Do this with every source of stress you wrote down. Motivation is an important feeling. It determines not only what you will change but how well you will tackle it.

The sources of stress that score high need to be the ones you tackle first. These will be the ones that will bring you the most satisfaction to alter. Significant sources of stress will be the primary explanation for your symptoms. Severe symptoms are a good reason to want to change things!

This is a significant source of stress; it will fuel your symptoms and needs you to act!

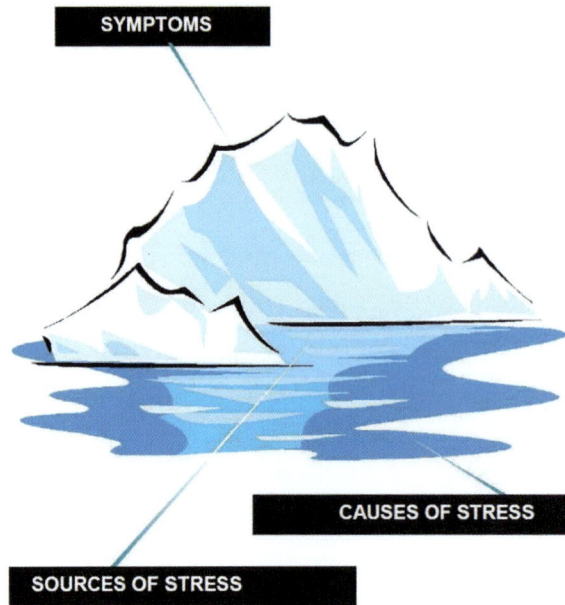

I liken this process to an iceberg. Above the surface, is a large piece of ice that is like your symptoms. Everyone can see them. They are the physical, mental, or emotional result of the difficulties in your life.

Below the surface is what's happening to you or the sources of your stress. These are the situations you experience that result in your symptoms. We can all hide up to a point, but some tension may be obvious, or we tend to 'let it out at home'.

Even deeper are the 'causes' of our stress or our thoughts and feelings about things. It is these underlying fears that influence our thoughts and what we do. Our values, past experiences, feelings and beliefs all influence our attitude to events. They become our 'filter'. Those situations we care about most can affect us the deepest. Whereas something we care about less is unlikely to stress us. The definition is:

A cause of stress is defined as an internal thought, feeling or reaction.

This is the biggest single key to our stress. Our thoughts about situations we experience, whether positive or negative are important. We can generate coping mechanisms this way or exacerbate our feelings. It can be as simple as saying 'I can do this' rather than 'I cannot do this' but that doesn't make it easy for us to alter. If we were able to think well about everything we did or experienced in life, then we would *feel* better too. To do this we must feel good about ourselves. Only then can we react to everything we meet so that we stay positive. We need to either be positive about our chances of problem solving a solution, or that it will all be ok.

This is why the sentence *"It's not what happens to us but how we react that matters"* is so important. Stress is an inside job and the remedy for stress is action!

Causes of stress are fewer in number than sources and there is one simple reason for this. Our experiences can be plenty but our thoughts are often the same. We may not be *aware* of having these thoughts, but we generate them. Our thoughts are very powerful triggers. A source of stress for one individual can different for another. For example, one man may be willing to jump off a bridge on a bungee whilst another would find that frightening. This is due to our thoughts.

Modern day living is very different from the life we had as primitive man. At that time, we needed adrenaline to escape. So, the mere sight of an animal could trigger the ability to fight for our lives or flee. Now we use gadgets for everything we do. From mobiles to computers, cars to trains, juicers to microwaves. Everything we use and every situation we find ourselves in, is different from the threats we faced as early man. This part of our brain has not evolved much since that time. What it means is that we are vulnerable. Stress is a normal everyday part of modern life but much of it comes from inside our own heads!

We can have common *sources* of stress. For example, moving house, death, or divorce are normal sources of stress. We are all likely to feel unhappy by these events. There are also specific sources of stress for us. In other words, experiences that people respond to in an individual way. The only thing that makes them different is our thoughts. Whether two people think the same thing about an event, or different things.

Common *causes* of stress are when we repeat the same perceived doubts about ourselves. Self-doubt is one of the biggest triggers of stress as is low self-esteem. For an Executive, the single biggest cause of stress I see is fear of failure.

Example Causes of Stress

Low self-esteem	Fear of failure
Self-doubt	Fear of rejection
Low self-worth	Fear of inadequacy
Low self-respect	Being competitive
Poor self-belief	Insecurity
Poor self-image	Guilt
Perfectionism	Fear of the unknown

These causes are all thoughts - either about you, people, situations, or events. Every thought and many others like them, could contribute to your stress. For example, the desire to be liked might be a fear of rejection.

Why do I get stressed?

As soon as you ask the question *why* something affects or bothers you, you are tapping in to the causes of your stress. *Why* asks the question, 'why' is it an issue for you?

Why situations or people trouble you is important. The more you identify how you feel about things and why you are feeling this way, the better. You can then tackle your thoughts.

When you ask this question be honest. Identifying that you fear failure or rejection is significant. If you're not sure of the correct cause of stress for you, taking what you do know to a therapist is an ideal way to begin.

One More Way to Recognise Your Causes of Stress

There is one more way to recognise what your personal causes of stress are. That is to look at the comfort zone and what it is. Our comfort zone serves a purpose. It is a belief that something we do in life is easier. We often enjoy being in it because we are capable and comfortable.

Staying within your comfort zone for too long can make us feel bored and under-stimulated. In my experience, Execs enjoy being out of their comfort zone, in fact they often seek to live out of it for long periods. This can make it difficult to recognise stress. They are *already* operating outside of their comfort zone. So, this behaviour can become the norm. Knowing your limits helps you say 'no' to excessive demands, or something that doesn't feel right for you.

Many Executives I speak to recognise that they feel attracted to a role that is stressful. The impact of this needs managing if they are to thrive. Otherwise, they can hide their stress and not deal well with it.

Overwhelm happens for an Executive when they feel they are not in control. They lack confidence with it or they may be unfamiliar or it's unexpected, so it is difficult to plan a solution. Also, if they are not in that situation by choice. For example, managing a merger that they don't want or agree with, can also be stressful. Then they may stop coping well. Executives tend to persevere so it can be a long time before they acknowledge, accept, or seek support.

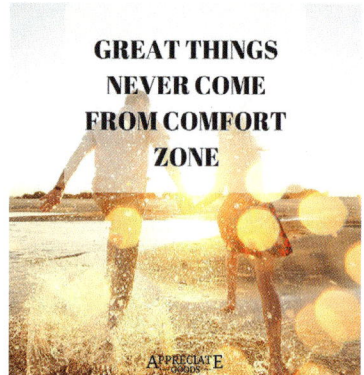

To Recap: *Underneath the way you react to every source of stress is the way you think about it. Critical to the way you think is what you think is what/ how you think about yourself. People who like themselves are less stressed. This is because they are more tolerant of everything they do. They aim for success and they tolerate their mistakes.*

Recommendations for Handling the Sources of Stress

In the earlier part of the chapter I described how it is necessary to identify your sources of stress. Then i suggested you get specific about what is the exact problem. Once you've done that, it's time to look at what you can do about sources of stress. These techniques fall roughly in to three options:

1. Can you adapt in any way?

Much of the time we don't like the message that we may have contributed to a situation that is bothering us. It can be tough to recognise we have to be the one to do something about it. It is human nature to avoid conflict and like to be right. So often it feels uncomfortable tackling difficult situations. Taking responsibility for ourselves and our feelings is critical to managing our stress. Even if it forces us out of our comfort zone to do it. Being the one to explain ourselves or change the way we are approaching a task **is the key** to feeling better.

When you have some uninterrupted time, sit down and think about what you can do to change a situation. How you are going to do that? If it is a difficulty with a person, think about what you want to say. How you will put your point across? Practice inside your head before tackling it. It is difficult to see how you will resolve a situation unless you are direct some of the time.

2. Seeking advice

Asking for support can come in many forms. In the scenario above it could be helpful to have someone act as a sounding board. This is because we can often make mistakes in being too aggressive or irritable. We often let our emotions take over instead of being calm and expressing ourselves well. If you are in conflict with someone this can be even more likely. Running your problem by a colleague or asking them to listen while you practice is useful.

There comes a time, when friends and family may not be the best people to help. This is not a personal statement about them but more a reflection on the difficulty of the situation. If your symptoms are contributing to a sense that you want to withdraw from the world, be aware this is stress. Learning to recognise when you need professional help is important. Depression results in a deep sense of isolation for people as I explained. Often a depressed person doesn't want to socialise. They may personalise events and see situations that go wrong as their fault. Losing perspective like this is part of the effect long-term stress can have. A depressive may also re-run events in his or her head playing out how bad or useless they think they are or were. If this is you, it might be better to seek support.

Professional help need not be intimidating. You may find that counselling services are sometimes available from within an organisation. Options include private health care or an Employee Assistance Programme. They may not feel accessible if you are very senior. That is why outside help may feel more confidential. Many companies *are* taking responsibility for stress and offer stress management support.

If you are able to access these services they are usually accessed over the telephone. They may also offer face to face meetings but these are voluntary. Other options include CRUSE which is a bereavement care organisation. It is a charity. You can contact them for anything to do with grief counselling on 0808 808 1677. They will tell you how to find your nearest counsellor.

If you want to pay for a counsellor look them up in the British Association of Counselling Practitioners (BACP). Even the yellow pages will list counsellors but you look for the letters BACP after their names. An initial consultation can cost you approximately £100.

Psychologists are available on the NHS in some primary health care trusts. To find a psychologist who can help you ask at your G.P. practice. There may be one in your geographical area. You could also visit your local library. They will keep the Directory of Chartered Psychologists. They list according to professional expertise and geographical area. Try to see a Clinical or Business Psychologist for problems of this sort.

3. Can the situation adapt in any way?

When we are in the middle of stressful situations it can be difficult to 'see the wood from the trees. We can feel overwhelmed by situations and unable to see a solution. The best thing to do is sit down and assess the problem. Aim to get some perspective on it. How much of the difficulty lies with you? Take a look at the pie chart below. Think of a percentage out of 100 that indicates how much you might be responsible for this? How much of the situation is the result of circumstances you find yourself in? How much involves other people and how much is out of your control completely? All these different aspects need different solutions.

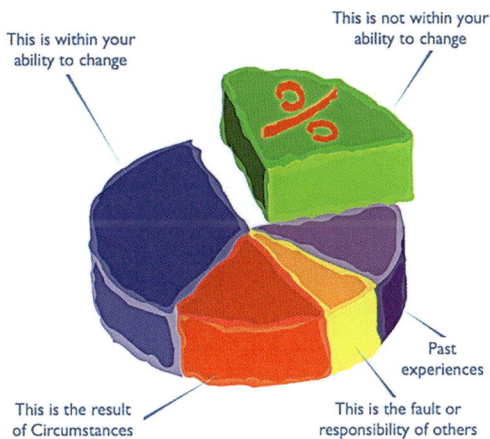

Each segment of this pie chart is something you need to tackle. Do anything and everything you can to change how you approach something or someone. What can you control rather than what you can't? Other people are not within our control but we can change or alter our thoughts about them.

Past experiences have a bearing on what you may be having difficulty with now. You might have a good reason to mistrust people. Situations that went wrong in the past leave us with doubts. These can be doubts related to unreliable people or those that have not treated us well.

Whatever you decide you will see what you can and cannot tackle. There is a famous saying that is invaluable for this situation:

"God grant me the serenity to determine what is within my control, what is not within my control and the wisdom to know the difference."
—St. Francis of Assisi

4. Can I avoid it?

The final section of these recommendations is can you avoid any aspect? Avoidance is not an easy let-out; it is often an act of self-preservation. If you had to travel to work by tube, for example, and you hated it, look for alternatives. Take the train or block out the experience of being on the tube, such as reading a book or listening to an audio book.

To recap, try to look at each source of stress you experience. Decide if there is any aspect of it you can change. Communicate better, change your approach, alter the situation itself or avoid it altogether.

Other Tips for Handling Sources

There are other techniques that might help when trying to achieve stress reduction. A few of these are here to give you food for thought.

1. Don't put things off

Depending on your personality, you may like to put things off. You want to get to them later or you think you work better under pressure. Putting things off can trigger a sense of inadequacy in you that adds to the tension of your day rather than aids it. We all have to prioritise the tasks we set ourselves in a day. We seem to put several further down the list until they appear to drop off it as they never get done! This is normal, but not doing certain jobs or tasks suggests the task might be enormous. One trick I like to use is to break a task down.

Ben Sweetland in his book 'I will' described that we are more effective if we break things down. Make each minor goal your major one. Reward yourself when each minor goal is complete. Reward is fundamental to achievement but taken for granted. Make a list of things you enjoy. Aim to reward yourself with one of these each time you achieve something significant to you.

2. Planning

Although this may seem obvious, I was once asked to comment on planning as a useful tool to prevent stress. I was stood on the side of a motorway slip road talking to a journalist. They were interviewing me about how to cope better with difficult journeys. I described how people often set out on a long journey. They take for granted their chances of achieving it in time and without mishap. In fact, it is all too common that an accident or road closure prevent you from reaching your destination. The value of planning seems obvious but we don't do the obvious. How many times do we write ourselves a list of things to do? We expect to achieve them all and then blame ourselves when we don't get them done?

Planning ahead is a useful tool but one that takes time. We are all so driven that we forget. It pays off though. Large organisations that change a service, provide a list of questions and answers at the back of the literature they send out. They plan in advance the problems someone might come across and include the answers. What can you do that helps you plan better?

Point of Interest

If you find you are not making a difference to your stress then it's possible you need to work with your causes of stress. Like the iceberg I referred to earlier, we are more complicated and deeper than we often realise. Our personality plays a very important part in the experience of stress. It's possible this is the better tactic for you. Many Executives I work with have fewer difficulties with the sources of stress. Their issue is often the cause of their negative thinking.

Recommendations for Handling the Causes of Stress

1. Self-talk or the internal chat inside our heads, is very significant. This is because self-talk relates to self-esteem and our 'estimation of ourselves'. This in turn, governs whether we can do something or whether we can't. In fact, it can feel as if there are two heads inside us at times.

It is easy to forget that these voices are within. We interpret them as if someone else is speaking. We can even believe the opinion of others above our own.

We all need to watch our self-talk. Pay attention to how many times you put yourself down if you are to control your fears. Start to appreciate how you talk to yourself and how it makes you feel.

To change your self-talk, it is important to recognise whether your self-esteem is low. We all take knocks in life but if these knocks have damaged you then you may have many self-doubts. It can become more difficult to be positive about yourself. There are many books on the market worth reading and some of these I recommend at the back of this book. This diagram represents self-esteem.

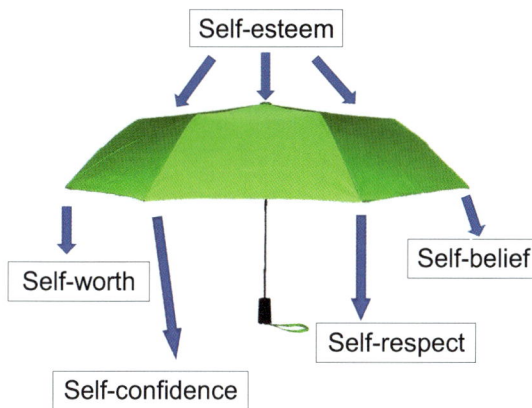

I refer to the fabric of the umbrella as representing self-esteem. It is at the root of our opinion of ourselves. The spokes of the umbrella are the support mechanism. They symbolize our different views of ourselves. Self-image, is how you look in the mirror. Do you like yourself? Many of us don't like that view and confuse uncertainty about body image with our self-worth. Self-worth is about how much we value ourselves. Often, we remain in relationships that are doing some damage to our self-esteem. Yet because we under-value ourselves it takes more courage to leave than it does to stay.

Self-confidence is about how we project ourselves to the outside world. Confident people seem to be able to do anything. In fact, they believe in themselves and project that belief in what they say and do. Belief is about conviction in your strengths. Self-awareness is about knowing yourself well. This is both strengths and weaknesses. Self-respect refers to liking yourself - regardless of how many strengths or weaknesses you have.

Self-doubt can afflict us in any area. This is like having a hole in the fabric. The hole lets in the rain and rots the fabric so that the hole gets bigger.

Recognising which part has suffered damage is important. You *can* repair it. Receiving feedback is uncomfortable. If the feedback you get you don't like, it is possible that that the criticism stung. With effort you can re-think this. Either accept it, do something about it, or communicate that you don't like it.

Self-esteem is the fabric that holds the spokes together. It serves a pivotal role in your defence mechanism against life's knocks. If nothing had knocked you in life then that might be great. You'd have a very positive sense of yourself and never feel unhappy. This isn't realistic though. Events in childhood, and adulthood shape your thinking and your attitude to authority. We do not question what people say to us as children, and this can leave us vulnerable to believing what adults say. Critical teachers, family members, even people in the street who want to have a 'dig' leave their mark. To repair self-esteem and prevent negative self-talk requires effort.

2. Personal coaching is one of the most effective methods of tackling low self-esteem. Coaches come in a variety of forms. Life coaches, executive coaches, and personal advisers such as myself. None of us are counsellors. You could try any of these to see if they help. Then consider counselling if there is a very deep-rooted issue.

They all approach the subject from the same angle. They will ask what are the issue/s, and how are they affecting you? What do you want to change? Then they offer a set of tools, tips, or guidelines to apply that result in improvement. The benefits are a targeted, personal approach. This is private. No-one knows you have been to see someone. You could also use a video call these days. I use Zoom/ Skype so that I can split the screen. This helps me show pictures, PowerPoint, and even write notes. This helps the client see visuals of my ideas or thoughts.

3. I have already mentioned counselling. It is the best method for helping someone change entrenched views. Poor self-esteem is often the result of more than one event in our past. It is likely that on-going support from a counsellor is valuable for intense experiences. These include abuse, alcoholism, depression, and the more extreme symptoms of stress.

4. It can help to read as much information on stress as you can. Books and CDs on the subject help. They can identify which events in your past have made you competitive, or perfectionist. Or to fear experiences. All these reactions are common causes of stress. Books on Cognitive Behavioural Therapy are valuable. So are those on the science of Neuro Linguistic Programming. There are some recommended titles in the bibliography at the back.

5. Overcoming the fear of failure is important for many people. As a quick guide but not an exhaustive one, your main aim is to recognise the following points:

    a. Failure is an emotive word. It conjures up images of a dejected individual who has never and will never be worth anything. Avoid using the word if you can. Refer to 'making mistakes, errors of judgement or a lack of success' instead.

    b. *Everyone* makes mistakes at some time in their lives.

    c. Mistakes are a delay in your success. If your goal was realistic in the first place and you have the motivation then re-set the goal again.

    d. If you feel you've failed, then decide to write down

        (i) What happened?

        (ii) What part did you play?

        (iii) What part did others play? iv.

        (iv) What can you do about it?

        (v) Now re-set the goal and try again!

6. Rejection is another significant cause of stress that I find is common. Follow this guideline to help give you an alternative perspective if this is your issue.

a. Rejection is only a measure of your self-worth if you choose to let it be.

b. Don't be subjective. Personalising every event as if life revolves around you can make you paranoid. If there is something you can change do. If that is a feature of your personality you may not be able to change this. Why should you? If it's an approach to a task, don't take on a sense of inadequacy as if you 'should' or 'ought' to be better than you are.

c. Don't overvalue someone else's viewpoint. Rejection of an idea is not rejection of you as a person

d. Review the assumptions you are making as opposed to the facts. Stick to the facts of a situation within something someone says. It is the assumptions we make that often stress us. We may be confusing *how* someone expressed something with what they *meant* to say. Few people in life are diplomatic. Many mistakes are in what some-one says even if their intentions were good.

7. A final 'fear' that is common is the fear of maintaining your own success. This is different from the fear of failure. Often the problem successful entrepreneurs have is how do they maintain their success? If this feels familiar bear the following suggestions in mind:

a. Will you always have the capacity to keep yourself or earn a living? It's likely that you will because everyone I ever meet is very driven to do well. You have skills, determination, drive and often intense desire to do well. These push you so any time you aren't doing as well as you like you'll try again.

b. Who sets the standards that you aim to reach? You do. Although you may have outdated standards set for you by parents if you run a family owned business. This can alter. Seek support to 'reframe' how you view things. This can ease the tension their expectations create in you.

c. Review your measure of success. Your desires, and your well-being must include the pursuit of your goals. Be realistic about what you want - not a perfectionist. Have some 'Big Audacious Goals' but have a sense of perspective that it is usually you who has to want these enough. You have achieved everything so far so there is nothing to say you will not find a way to help yourself in the future.

d. Feed' your self-talk with positive results of your success in the past. Look back at the exercise in chapter 4 and keep a gratitude journal that records what you've done. This is vital to remind you of what you *can* do rather than what you *think you can't.*

Remember self-appreciation not self-deprecation!

In Conclusion

Stress is in your body, but it starts in your mind! The causes of stress are the most significant thing I have mentioned in this book. It is vital to recognise your causes of stress. Acknowledge that they exist, accept them and if appropriate, do something. It takes time and courage to change the way you think about yourself. It is worthwhile though. If you can reduce the tension, unhappiness or distress you may be causing yourself in your life do it. You're worth it!

Eleanor Roosevelt once said: *"If you think you can or you think you can't, you'll always be right"*

She was a bright woman and she was right!

My very best wishes to you all,

Susan Firth BSc, MSc, AFBPsS, CPsychol
Business Psychologist, Stress expert, author & speaker
www.suefirthltd.com

ABOUT SUE FIRTH

Sue Firth is a Business Psychologist, Stress Expert & a leading authority on Stress and Managing Change. She is also an Author and is a specialist in helping CEOs and senior executives manage stress, from an individual and group perspective. She is an international speaker & presenter and holds both a Batchelor of Science and a Master's Degree. She is a member of the British Psychological Society and The Health Professions Council.

During the course of her work she enables people to increase self-esteem and confidence by removing negative thoughts and changing long-held damaging self-belief traits. Her style is engaging, motivating, sensitive and down-to-earth. Her refreshing approach and techniques are unsurpassed. Sue helps individuals and businesses become more productive, purposeful, successful and profitable.

She works with a number of high-profile corporate clients

To book Sue for coaching or speaking
please consult her website www.suefirthltd.com

BIBLIOGRAPHY

Agness, Lindsey.
Change your life with NLP: The powerful way to make your life better.
Prentice Hall

Canfield, Jack.
How to Get from Where You Are to Where You Want to Be.
Harper Element

Charlton, Bruce.
Psychiatry and the Human Condition.
Abingdon, Oxfordshire, England: Radcliffe Medical Press Ltd, 2000

Church, Matt.
Adrenaline Junkies and Serotonin Seekers.
Ulysses Press

Firth, Susan.
Taking the Stress Out of Life'
CD and audio download available from www.suefirthltd.com

Firth, Susan.
Tap into Your Potential, Maximise Your Self-esteem
CD available from www.suefirthltd.com

Gill, Jill.
Stress Survival Guide.
London: HarperCollins

Goldsmith, Marshall.
What Got You Here Won't Get You There.
Profile Books

Hanson, Peter.
The Joy of Stress.
London: Pan Books Ltd,

Johnson, Dr Spencer.
Who Moved My Cheese?
U.S. Simon & Schuster,

Rowe, Dorothy.
Depression: The Way Out of Your Prison.
London: Routledge and Kegan Paul

Sharma, Robin.
The Monk Who Sold His Ferrari.
Harper Element

Stuttaford, Dr Tom.
Stress and How to Avoid It.
London: Little Books Ltd,

Webber, Christine.
Get the Self-esteem Habit.
Hodder & Stoughton,

USEFUL CONTACTS

Alcohol-Related Problems

Alcoholics Anonymous
0800 9177 650

Al-Anon and Alateen (for families)
0207 403 0888

Careers Advisers

www.johnlesscareers.com

Children

Family Lives
Helpline: +44 (0) 808 8002222

Counselling

British Association of Counselling
+44 (0) 1455 883300

British Psychotherapy Foundation
+44 (0) 208 452 9823

British Psychological Society
+ 44 (0)116 254 9568

The National Council
of Psychotherapists
+44 (0) 800 170 1250

Death and Bereavement

Cruse Bereavement Care
+44 (0) 808 808 1677

Debt Sorting

0800 002 9051

Depression

MIND (National Association
for Mental Health)
Info line: +44 (0) 208 519 2122

Divorce

Gingerbread
+ 44 (0) 207 428 5400

Eating Disorders

Eating Disorders Association
Helpline: 0845 838 2040

Financial Problems

Citizens Advice Bureau
03444 111 444

Hypnosis

National Council for Hypnotherapy
0800 980 4419

Meditation

www.how-to-meditate.org

Infertility

Infertility network UK
01424 732361

Menopause

The Amarant Trust
(menopause and HRT)
Advice line: +44 (0) 207 401 3855

Miscarriage

The Miscarriage Association
+44 (0) 1924 200799

Naturopathy

College of Naturopathic Medicine
+ 44 (0) 1342 410 505

Panic Attacks and Phobias

Panic Attacks and Anxiety
+44 (0) 208 519 2122

Personal Coaches

www.lifecoach.com

Public Speaking

www.thepsa.co.uk

Redundancy

www.newlifenetwork.co.uk

Relationships

Relate
0300 100 1234

Retirement

Age Concern
0800 055 6112

Stress Management

www.suefirthltd.com
58 South Molton St, London
ISMA (International Stress Management Association)
www.isma.org.uk

Printed in Great Britain
by Amazon